The RICE COOKER'S COMPANION

Japanese American Food and Stories

National Japanese American Historical Society

Proceeds from the sale of this cookbook will go toward the programs of the National Japanese American Historical Society.

The information contained in this book is accurate and complete to the best of our knowledge. Recipes were tested in the homes of our contributing members, friends, and family of the Cookbook Committee and the National Japanese American Historical Society. All recommendations are made without guarantees.

Library of Congress Cataloging-in-Publication Data

The Rice Cooker's Companion: Japanese American Food and Stories.
1. Japanese American—Culture. I. Nishikawa, Gayle T.
ISBN 1-881506-09-6
99-076749

Text and cover design by Dana Nakagawa, Gordon Chun Design
Publication production by Mango Press

Table of Contents

We dedicate this book to Yaye Herman
whose original idea of a cookbook was to share our stories and recipes in an
effort to build a stronger community through food and good nutrition.

NATIONAL JAPANESE AMERICAN HISTORICAL SOCIETY

The National Japanese American Historical Society (NJAHS) is a non-profit organization dedicated to the preservation, promotion, and dissemination of materials relating to the history and culture of the Japanese American experience. NJAHS develops and presents exhibitions, videos, publications, interactive multimedia and public programs of the historical events, personalities, arts, and cultural crafts of the Japanese American community.

Founded in 1980 as Go For Broke, the organization's purpose was to tell the story of the military exploits of the 100th/442nd Regimental Combat Team in Europe. In 1983, NJAHS expanded its mission and scope, changed its name to the National Japanese American Historical Society (NJAHS), and tells the entire story of the Japanese American experience. NJAHS has developed exhibitions in collaboration with such museums as The Oakland Museum of California, the Smithsonian Institution, the Smithsonian Institution Traveling Exhibition Services, and the Bishop Museum in Hawai'i. It coordinated the collection of artifacts for the Smithsonian Institution's special exhibit, *A More Perfect Union, Japanese Americans and the U.S. Constitution.* In 1990, it co-sponsored, with The Oakland Museum, *Strength & Diversity: Japanese American Women, 1885–1990,* which showcased the historical, social, and artistic endeavors of Japanese American women. Performances, films, videos, and literary artists were presented in the community collaboration. The exhibition won accolades from the Smithsonian Institution and the American Association for State and Local History. In 1997, two of its exhibits, *Reminiscing in Swingtime: Japanese Americans in American Popular Music* and *Diamonds in the Rough: Japanese Americans in Baseball* were shown at the Herbst International Exhibition Hall in the Presidio of San Francisco.

In May 1997, NJAHS became a Park Partner with the National Park Service/Golden Gate National Recreation Area to interpret jointly the Japanese American experience at the Presidio of San Francisco. Together with the Military Intelligence Service Association of Northern California, NJAHS is working with the Presidio Trust and the National Park Service to preserve Building 640 at Crissy Field, which was the original site of the secret language school for Japanese American linguists during World War II.

The CD-ROM, *Children of the Camps: An American Story of Civil Liberties,* funded in part by a grant from the Civil Liberties Public Education Fund. The project was completed in the summer of 1999 and currently is available for distribution. Historical community tours are led bi-annually to introduce participants to the life and culture of Japanese Americans in California.

FOREWORD

It is certainly appropriate that the National Japanese American Historical Society has chosen to put together a cookbook as a historical document.

I've often wondered if Japanese Americans are unusually food-obsessed. The answer, I think, is yes. Remarkably so, given the fact that we're not particularly vexed by weight problems. My theory is that we can afford to be food obsessed because we're choosy about the quality of the food we eat, and we also expend a lot of energy finding, fixing and fussing over the food.

But food is not just physical nourishment. It has many levels of meaning for us as a people. For instance:

Immigrant roots and making do: The issei, and sometimes older nisei, especially in areas where there were few Japanese, were unable to get many accustomed Japanese foodstuffs and at the same time confronted unfamiliar foods, such as canned tuna and hamburger. They therefore innovated, incorporating local "American" ingredients into Japanese dishes, leading to such concoctions as "hamburger sukiyaki" and "shōyu hotdogs" or combining Japanese and American elements in one meal, leading to combinations such as corned beef and cabbage with rice. I know that I was surprised to discover that other people ate potatoes with corned beef and cabbage. Additionally, over the years we nikkei have adapted to the regions in which we found ourselves. For example, in Hawaii, we incorporated Hawaiian, Chinese, Korean, and Portuguese elements to come up with the now-famous "plate lunch." In New England, we learned to make smoked turkey, and in Chicago, to chop up Vienna hot-dogs into our fried rice.

Generational continuity and change: The preparing and eating of certain foods has been passed down from generation to generation. Some of these dishes were common to most Japanese, but many were specialties of the regions from which our forebears came, Okinawa, Hiroshima, Kumamoto or wherever. For sansei, our memories of grandparents is associated with particular dishes that we ate at jichan and bachan's house or that they prepared for us when they visited. Many of the recipes in this book are of that sort. On the other hand, changes in food preference also mark generational changes; some of the dishes that our grandparents liked are no longer in vogue, either because they don't appeal to our taste buds (mochi) or because they don't seem very healthy (remember steamed pork fat?). In turn, new inventions with a Japanese touch, such as "sōmen salad" or "tōfu quiche" that our grandparents would not recognize, have been added to our repertoire.

Generosity and communal ties: Bringing dishes for family, church/temple functions, kenjinkai suppers and picnics has been a way of sharing (and sometimes showing off!). Most of us remember the huge plates of sushi, teriyaki chicken, salads and other dishes brought by each family to contribute to these events. At the end, there would be enough to feed everyone again, so we each took plates of leftovers made up of bits from all of the platters her relatives prepared for special occasions, especially New Year. In addition to chicken, sashimi, tempura, and sushi, there were dishes that appeared only once a year: baked fish tied to look as though it were leaping, ozōni, kuromame, and umani, and no Okinawan New Year was complete without pig's feet soup, andagii, and various pork dishes. Sometimes we ate out, and when we did, "China-meshi" was the cuisine of choice, and certain occasions—weddings, funerals, birthdays, and anniversaries—were observed with a banquet at a local Chinese restaurant. Old-time "China-meshi favorites included chow mein, pressed duck, and sweet and sour spare ribs. Today, we're more likely to have Peking duck, General Gau's chicken, and steamed fish, washed down with ginger-ale or bubbly apple cider.

I have written a lot of this in the past tense, but the themes remain valid, even if the specific foods and practices have changed over the years. The cookbook editors have admirably captured the diversity and richness of Japanese American food traditions.

—Evelyn Nakano Glenn

Acknowledgments

COOKBOOK COMMITTEE MEMBERS

The following have given freely of their time, talents, and energies to produce and promote *The Rice Cooker's Companion: Japanese American Food and Stories:*

Gayle Nishikawa
Editor

Patricia Abe Calef
Kiku Funabiki
Evelyn Nakano Glenn, Ph.D.
Judy Hamaguchi
Valerie Ito
Dana Kawaoka
Karen Leong
Jennifer Matsumura
Norman Masuda

Mariko Miho
Ernita O'Brien
Dianne Yamashiro-Omi
Lois Ohwa
Valerie Tanaka
Rosalyn Tonai
Lisa Hirai-Tsuchitani, Ph.D.
gayle yamada
Donald Yamamoto
Lisa Yamashiro
Sharon Yow

Volunteers:
Eiko Akama
Tomomi Kosaka
Rose Oda
Masa Satow
Bette Takeshita

Thank you to the staff of the National Japanese American Historical Society for their support of this project:

Rosalyn Tonai
Executive Director

Sathya Seigel
Program Manager

Meredith Oda
Projects and Research

Gary Otake
Computer Assistance

Jo Morohashi
Collections Manager

CONTRIBUTORS

Special thanks to our contributors who made the production of this book possible.
We apologize for any unintentional omissions.

Corporate Sponsors
Kikkoman International
JFC International

Business Sponsors
Hokubei Mainichi
Kariyushi Kai
MIF Insurance Agency
Moriwaki, Imai, and Fujita, Inc.
Oakland Asian Cultural Agency
David Pietsch, Jr.
Title Guaranty of Hawai'i, Inc.

Individual Sponsors
Roy Abe
Shizu & Raymond Aka
Natsuko Akiyama
Anonymous
Jean Arase
Mr. & Mrs. Hiroshi Arisumi
Fumi Ashizawa
Joyce Ashizawa-Yee
Mineko Sasahara Avery
Bentley Family
E. Keith Brown & Co.
Yasunori Deguchi
Dianna K. Eaton
Helen Yorozu Erlandson
Yukiye Fong
Toko Fujii
Sam & Teri Fujikawa
Mr. & Mrs. Peter Fukasawa
Dr. Minoru Fukuda
Harry Fukuhara
Dr. George M. Fukui
Nord & Sandy Gardner
Al & Kiyo Geron
Arthur Gorai
John Hamachi
Carolyn Hammerberg
Mariko Hanami
Kikuko Sue Hannel
Yoshino Hasegawa
Miriam Hatamiya
Fumi Manabe Hayashi

Clara T. Hayashi
Roy Hayashi
Yukiyo Hayashi
Steven T. Hayashi
Mrs. D. Y. Henjyoji
Jonathan Hirabayashi
Cathy Hiraga
Florence Hiraga
George & Lin Hirai
Bill & Ruth Hiraoka
Yo Hironaka
Brett & Brianna Hornig
Estella Hoshimiya
Rachel Hum
Mr. & Mrs. S. K. Ichiki
Chizu Iiyama
Satsuki Ina, Ph.D.
Jeanne Inase
Mr. & Mrs. Joseph Inatome
Mino & Kathy Inoshita
Fusae Ippongi
Natsuko Irei
L. & R. Ishihara
Fumiko Isobe
Naoko Ito
Shirley Ito
Tomi Ito
Kent Iwamiya
Toshiko Mary Iwamoto
Daniel Iwasaki
Nami Iwataki
Japanese American Services of
   the East Bay
Emy Kuroda Kada
Susan Kai
Ken Kaji
Mihako Kajiyama
Rodger T. Kame, O.D.
Milton T. Kanatani
Ann Kanazawa
Wayne M. Kanemoto
Tosh Kasai
Kiyoshi & Emiko Katsumoto
Sudi Sadako Kawaguchi
Jane & Harry Kawahara

Edward E. Kawahara
Hanako F. Kawamoto
Maureen Kawaoka
George Kitahara Kich
Sharon Kinoshita
George & Ikuko Kiriyama
Sharon S. Kitagawa
Hideo Kiyomura
Kazuo Kiyomura
Alicia Knust
Mr. & Mrs. Kazumi Kondo
Jeanne Matsumiya Konishi
Irene F. Koseki
Robert Koshiyama
Kiyo F. Kuroda
Marti Masumi Kuroda
Harry H. Kutara
Florice Kuwahara
Karen Leong
Carrie Machida
May Manabe
Kazuo Maruoka
Kayoshi Masuoka
Kazuko Matsumoto
Hiroshi (Hiro) Mayeda
May S. Mayeda
Marna Miikizior
Minami, Lew, & Tamaki
Congresswoman Patsy T. Mink
Doris S. Mita
Ray & Suzie Miyamoto
Renee Miyashiro-Devone
Doris H. Miyashita
Lynn Miyazaki
Atsuko Moriuchi
Donna Mukogawa
Mrs. Ryo Munekata
Victor Muraoka
Kenji Murase
Mr. & Mrs. Sam Musashi
Dr. Carl & Janice Muto
Art & Ann Muto
Lionel & Kathleen Nagata
Irene I. Nagata
Alice Nakahata

Louise Nakamura
John & Sally Nakao
Sumi K. Nakashima
Lorry M. Nakatsu
Kayoko Nakauchi
Mr. & Mrs. William Nicholson
Nobuo Nishi
Gayle T. Nishikawa
Jeannette Nishikawa
Kiyoshi & Emiko Nishikawa
Judi Nishimine
Arthur and Gloria Nishioka
Nancy Nishioka
Yvonne H. Noguchi
Akira & Yulie Nose
Esther Oda
Craney Connie Ogata
Dolly Ogata
Tey Oji
Kim & Hiroko Okawachi
Yasuo Okinaka
Gilbert S. Onaka, M.D.
Gene & Christine Ono
Berdi Oshidari
Mrs. Hide Oshima
Yukisada Oshiro
Kazuma & Kikue Oyama
Fred & Lorraine Ryo
Barry and Yuriko Saiki
Irene Y. Saiki
Margaret Saito
Emiko Judy Saito
Mariko Sakahara
Fusako Sakai
Sam Sakai
Chieko Sakai
Thomas Sakamoto
Chizuko Sakuma
Emily Sano
Masa Satow
Janet & David W. Schein
Hitomi Sera
Dr. & Mrs. Seiji Shiba
Yoshimi & Grace Shibata
Matao Shigio
Chiyeko Shikuma

Toshiko Shimoura
Eucaly A. Shirai
Taka I. Sonoda
Mr. & Mrs. Tamio Azuma Spiegel
Mr. June Sunahara
Roy and Caryl Suzuki
Ayako Tagashira
Mrs. Mildred Taira
Kaz Takahashi
Lily Takahashi
Rita Takahashi, Ph.D.
Gerald Takano, A.I.A.
Taro Tom Takeda
Emiko Takusagawa
Minoru & Iyo Tamaki
Edith Tanaka
Walter & Kae Tanaka
Yuriko Tanamachi
Cecil Tange
Mrs. Betty Taniguchi
Takeko Tanisawa
Lawrence Tawa, M.D.
Sandra C. Taylor
Jane & Richard Togikawa
Joanne Kiyoko Tohei
Lorraine T. Tokimoto
Lynn & Kirr Tomioka
Kenji & Mary Tomita
Minoru & Mary Tonai
Rosalyn Tonai
Gail Tsuchimoto Beach
M. Tsukada
Chiyeko Tsukiji
Toshiko Tsurumaki, M.D.
Marvin & Miyo Uratsu
Kimiko Uto
Robert & Yasuko Utsumi
Clifford & Betty Uyeda
Kenji K. Uyesugi
Marion and Lloyd Wake
May Watanabe
Kay Willis
Roberta Wong
Bea & Chaney Wong
Mr. & Mrs. Craig Wood
Ken & Ann Yabusaki

George Yada
Kazuhiko Yamada
Jessica R. Yamada
Aiko M. Yamamoto
M. Yamamoto
Margie Yamamoto
Steve S. Yamamoto
Helen & Mas Yamasaki
Dianne Yamashiro-Omi
Sumika Yamashita
Gayle C. Yanagida
Margaret Yanagimachi
Noboru Yanagitani
Ralph Yasuoka
Mitsie Yatabe
Penelope S. Yip, D.D.S.
Motomi Yokomizo
Irene Yoshida
Takeshi Yoshida
Yoneo Yoshimura
Kiyo Yoshimura
Tomiyo Yoshiwaka
Tee Yoshiwara
H. J. Yoshizawa
Sharon Yow

Recipes have come from Japanese American communities across the country. We thank all our rice cookers and storytellers who have opened their recipes boxes and retold family tales for this book. We apologize for any unintentional omissions.

Lily Abiko, California
Janice Agena, Hawai'i
Norma U. Ah Tou, Hawai'i
Chiyeko Aoki, Colorado
Julia Estrella, Hawai'i
Karen Fujii, California
Kiku Funabiki, California
Evelyn Nakano Glenn, California
Iris Hiraga-Higgins, California
Catherine Hiraga, California
Kei Hiraga, California
Tsuyu Hiura, California
Fred and Setsu Hirasuna, California
Ann Hiyama, California
Yoshino T. Hasegawa, California
Shizue Ichinotsubo, Hawai'i
Aiko Imada, Indiana
Mariko Imada, Indiana
Sandra Inaba, California
Jean Ishibashi, California
Bernice Ito, California
Kaoru Ito, California
Naoko Ito, California
Shirley Ito, California
Susumu Ito, Massachusetts
Annette Iwahashi, Hawai'i
Yoshie Iwahashi, Hawai'i
Patsy Nakayama Iwasaki, Hawai'i
Chizu Iyama, California
Ken Kaji, California
Ellen Kamimoto, California
Hiroshi Kashiwagi, California
Lilly Kato, California
Maureen Kawaoka, California
Lucy Kishaba, California
Karen Kondo, California
Jean Konishi, Utah

Erika Kono, Illinois
Irene Kozuki. California
Florice Kuwahara, California
Norman Masuda, California
Jennifer Matsumura, Oregon
Doris Mita, Wisconsin
Janice Muto, California
Mary Mizono, California
Donna Mukogawa, Illinois
Kenji Murase, California
Ann Nagaki, Idaho
Gwen Nagata, Hawai'i
Irene Nagata, Hawai'i
Ruby Nakagawa, California
Lori Nakamura, Hawai'i
Mitsuko Nakamura, Illinois
Mei Nakano, California
Mei Nakano, Oregon
Kay Nakauchi, California
Jeannette Nishikawa, Hawai'i
Ernita O'Brien, California
Steven Oshiro, California
Yuki Otake, California
Jeanne Ozawa, Oregon
Palo Alto Buddhist Women's Association
Irene Saiki, California
Emma Saito, California
Emily Sano, California
Masa Satow, California
Seattle Betsuin Buddhist Women's Association
Hitomi Sera, California
Shizue Seigel, California
Stephen Murphy-Shigematsu, Massachusetts
Donna Hiraga-Stephens, California
Tami Suzuki, California

Linda Takemoto, Hawai'i
Tacoma Buddhist Women's Association
Karen Tani, California
Yoneyo Taniguchi, California
Mildred Taira, Hawai'i
Gerry Takano, California
Jo Takata, California
Suz H. Takeda, California
Linda Takemoto, Hawai'i
Edith Tanaka, California
Valerie Tanaka, Hawai'i
Karen Tani, California
Yoneyo Taniguchi, California
Jane Togikawa, Hawai'i
Sally Tokinaga, Hawai'i
Lois Tranilla, Hawai'i
M. Tsukada, Washington
Ellie Urakawa, Hawai'i
Kimi Uto, Hawai'i
Lloyd Wake, California
Marion N. Wake, California
Ann Yabusaki, California
K. Ken Yabusaki, California
Margaret Yanagimachi, Washington
The late Katsu Oikawa Yenari, Louisiana
Midori Yenari, California
Tee Yoshiwara, California
Namiko Yokoyama, California

Helpful Hints

ARAIMO (SATOIMO)

- Parboil araimo and peel skin for easier preparation.

- To prevent itchiness when peeling raw araimo, dip wet hands in salt or peel under running water.

AZUKI BEANS

- To retain red color in azuki, add ½ teaspoon baking soda to 4 cups water to cook rice and azuki for sekihan.

- To prepare azuki for zenzai, manjū, or mochi, soak in water, rinse, add fresh water, and continue cooking until beans are soft.

DAIKON

- Precooking cut daikon in shiro mizu (water with a handful of raw rice) will remove bitterness. Drain, rinse, and cook.

EGGS

- To prepare eggs for garnish, beat eggs with pinch of sugar and of salt. Fry in thin sheets and cut into short, fine strips. A few drops of sake will enhance the flavor.

FISH

- Buy cut fish that is firm, clean, with a fresh odor, translucent in color, and moist.

- Buy whole fish that has shiny, clear eyes. Gills should be bright red.

- Rub fish with lemon juice before cooking to reduce the odor and improve flavor.

- Soak fish fillets in milk half an hour before frying. This removes the odor and tenderizes the fish. Add salt after cooking.

- To prevent breakage when slicing fish, rub knife with cooking oil.

GOBŌ

- To prevent discoloration of gobō, scrape root with back of a knife, cut as desired, then soak 10 to 15 minutes in water with vinegar.

KANPYŌ

- Kanpyō can be cooked faster by first rinsing with water, rubbing with salt, then rinsing again.

KONNYAKU

- To soften konnyaku, sprinkle with salt and slap it on a cutting board several times; rinse and use.

MEATS

- When cooking meat or poultry, add sugar before salt or shōyu. Adding salt first toughens the meat.

- Coat slices of meat with oil before broiling or frying to prevent it from becoming dry.

MISO

- When miso is used in any dish, bring it to a boil and remove from heat immediately to retain its full flavor.

- A few drops of shōyu added to miso soup just before turning off the heat enhances the flavor. Soup is more flavorful if both red and white miso are used.

OKARA

- Dried okara is excellent in baked goods and can be used in place of bread or cracker crumbs.

- Dry okara by spreading it thinly on a cookie sheet and baking it at 250 degrees. It is done when it is creamy in color and dry to the touch.

- Wet okara keeps one week. Dry okara keeps indefinitely.

RENKON OR HASU

- Adding a little vinegar when boiling lotus root prevents discoloration.

SESAME SEEDS

- The flavor of sesame seeds is enhanced when you toast the seeds for 3 to 5 minutes in a skillet. Toss and stir constantly until seeds pop and turn brown.

- Toast sesame seeds with a screen cover to prevent seeds from flying.

SHIITAKE

- To soften shiitake, rinse and soak in warm water with a pinch of sugar for 15 to 20 minutes; cut into desired size. Save water for sauces, soup stock, and seasoning.

SUSHI

- Wash rice and cook in water with sake, salt, and konbu. Konbu may be left in or removed. When rice is done, transfer to hanbo or handai. Add awase zu and, using a shamoji, mix well with a horizontal cutting motion, constantly fanning to cool rice (an electric fan is helpful).

- One cup of rice makes 4 musubi.

- Sushi must be made fresh but nori, shiitake, and kanpyō can be cooked ahead and frozen.

- Rinse hanbo or handai just before using for sushi to prevent sticking.

- When slicing sushi, wipe knife blade with a damp cloth or run it through an orange to prevent sticking.

TENPURA

- Good tenpura is light. Do not overmix the batter. Add ice cubes to the batter to lighten the texture.

- To get a lacy shrimp, use a lighter batter. Sprinkle a little batter into hot oil with fingers. Lay battered shrimp on the sprinkled batter. Sprinkle more batter on and around shrimp.

TŌFU

- Tōfu is best fresh, but you can store it in a bowl of clean, cold water. It can be refrigerated up to a week by changing the water every day.

- Another method of storing tōfu is to boil tōfu to make it firm and keep longer. Another suggestion is to simmer in water 3 to 4 minutes before storing in water.

- Soak tōfu in salted water for a while to prevent tōfu from crumbling.

EATING WELL

DAIRY

- Replace a whole egg with 2 egg whites or an egg substitute.
- Use non-fat milk.
- Sour cream can be replaced with fat-free or low-fat yogurt.
- Use cottage cheese instead of ricotta cheese.

MEATS/SEAFOOD

- Select lean cuts of meat; trim visible fat. Remove skin and fat from poultry.
- Refrigerate, then skim fat from stews, soups, and gravies.
- Bake, broil, grill, poach, or microwave meat, poultry, or fish instead of frying it in fat.
- When browning meat, eliminate fat by using a nonstick pan or cooking spray; some fat will come from the meat as it cooks.
- Using lemon juice and rind in the water for poached fish will keep the fish firm and add flavor.
- Use ground chicken or turkey instead of ground beef or pork.

OILS

- Use vegetable cooking sprays instead of butter, margarine, or oil.
- Replace some or all of the oil in quick breads by using applesauce or mashed bananas.

SEASONINGS/SWEETENERS

- Eliminate monosodium glutamate. Most of us will not know the difference.
- Sugar or other sweeteners can be reduced by ¼ to ⅓ when preparing most baked goods.
- Paprika is a good subsitute for salt with baked or fried potatoes.
- Reduce the amount of shōyu by half or use a low soduim shōyu.

STARCHES

- Whole wheat flour can replace part or all of the all-purpose flour in most recipes; use 2 Tablespoons less per cup.
- Use dried okara instead of bread or cracker crumbs.

VEGETABLES

- Tōfu is high in protein, calcium, iron, zinc, and B-complex vitamins. It is also high in fat. Firm tōfu has the highest fat content.
- Tōfu can be frozen and used instead of ground meat or chicken. Frozen tōfu has a texture of ground meat. Squeeze water out of thawed tōfu and break into small pieces.

Eat Right to Lower High Blood Pressure For Japanese Americans

Developed by Lisa Yamashiro, R.D. *September, 1999*

GUIDELINE

1. Eat at least 2 to 3 servings of low-fat dairy products every day.

1 serving equals:
- 1 cup skim or 1% low-fat milk
- 1 cup low-fat yogurt
- 1.5 oz. cheese

Dairy foods are excellent sources of calcium.

COMMENTS

- Calcium not only keeps your bones strong but may also play a role in controlling high blood pressure.

- If milk gives you digestive problems, try smaller portions of milk with meals. Yogurt and cheese are often better tolerated. Or try a lactose-reduced milk.

HEALTHY CHOICES

- Skim or 1% milk, yogurt, or cheese

- Other good sources of calcium: tōfu, dark green vegetables, fish with edible bones such as canned salmon or sardines, calcium-fortified orange juice

---

GUIDELINE

2. Eat 8 to 10 servings of fruits and vegetables every day.

1 serving equals:
- 1 cup raw leafy greens
- ½ cup cooked vegetables, or fresh, frozen, or canned fruit
- 6 oz vegetable or fruit juice
- 1 medium fruit
- ¼ cup dried fruit

COMMENTS

- Eating more fruits and veggies can boost your potassium and magnesium intake, which may benefit blood pressure. They also provide plenty of other vitamins, minerals, and fiber for good health.

HEALTHY CHOICES

- Aim for 2 to 3 servings of fruits and vegetables with each meal. Try frozen or canned for convenience. Snack on fruits and vegetables. Add extra vegetables to soups, stews, one-pot, and stir-fried dishes. Enjoy fruit for dessert.

GUIDELINE

3. Eat LESS sodium.

Eat less processed "instant" foods.
Eat less cured or pickled foods.
Use less added salt.
Use other seasonings, spices, and herbs instead of salt. Your taste buds will adjust to less salt.

COMMENTS

- Cutting back on sodium can help lower your blood pressure and make your medications work better.
- When you eat a food high in sodium, balance that choice with foods that are lower in sodium. Remember it's the TOTAL amount of sodium you eat in a day that matters. Practice moderation when it comes to higher sodium foods.

- Remove salt shaker from table.
- Use low sodium soy sauce.
- Omit extra salt and MSG from recipes.
- Serve sauces "on the side."
- Don't drink the broth of noodle dishes.
- Read food labels carefully. Limit foods with %Daily Value for sodium >20%, to <1 serving per day.
- Spice it up with pepper, curry, garlic, ginger, herbs, shiso, lemon, vinegar, no salt furikake, shiitake, wasabi . . .

GUIDELINE

4. Eat LESS fat.
High blood pressure speeds up artery clogging, which can lead to heart attack or stroke.

COMMENTS
- Choose high fat foods less often. Find a lower fat alternative.
- Savor smaller portions.
- Change method of preparation.

HEALTHY CHOICES
- Limit lean meat portions to no more than 6 oz per day.
- Eat more fish and seafood.
- Use canola and olive oil in moderation.
- Eat fewer fried foods.

GUIDELINE

5. If you drink alcoholic beverages, do so in moderation.
If you don't drink, don't start.

COMMENTS
- Alcohol can raise your blood pressure and cause other serious health problems. Alcohol has a lot of calories and promotes overeating.

HEALTHY CHOICES
- Check with your doctor first.
- Men: <2 drinks a day   Women: <1 drink a day

GUIDELINE

6. Enjoy a physically active lifestyle.
Exercise is the BEST medicine!

COMMENTS
- Reduces risk of heart disease, lowers cholesterol, helps lower high blood pressure, reduces stress, helps weight loss, and makes you feel great!

HEALTHY CHOICES
- Check with your doctor first.
- Aim for at least 30 minutes daily. Walk, dance, golf, tennis . . . find an activity you enjoy regularly.

GUIDELINE

7. Lose weight if overweight.
Maintain a healthy weight.

COMMENTS
- Being overweight increases your chances of developing high blood pressure. Shedding extra pounds can bring your blood pressure down.

HEALTHY CHOICES
- Focus on healthy eating, NOT "dieting." Cut back on fat. Watch portion sizes!
- Increase physical activity.

GUIDELINE

8. STOP smoking.
For specific medical advice, consult with your physician or registered dietitian.

Tea & Dietary Benefits

By Clifford I. Uyeda, M.D.

In the 1970's, medical researchers started to take note of the strong anti-oxidant properties of green tea. Researchers are learning that Asians have benefited from a lower risk of many diseases that plague western countries. Dietary factors seem to contribute to this discrepancy, and the consumption of green tea ranks high as one of these factors. The tea-growing Shizuoka Prefecture of Japan has a much lower cancer death rate, including stomach cancer, for both men and women, than any other prefecture. People there drink more cups of green tea than other Japanese citizens.

A half-century ago, medical schools taught that breast cancer rarely occurred in Japanese women. Now, however, the breast cancer rate among nikkei women is about the same as for other American women. Researchers have found that green tea polyphenols appear beneficial in inhibiting the growth of breast tumors.

The benefits of green tea also appear to apply to men. Japanese men are twice as likely as American men to smoke, but the lung cancer mortality rates in Japan are lower than in the United States. Regular consumption of green tea, as well as other foods common in a Japanese diet, may provide some protection from the carcinogens in tobacco smoke.

Green tea may also be responsible for lowering the body's cholesterol levels and contributing to a lower rate of cardiovascular disease and strokes. The average intake of green tea in Asian countries is about three cups daily, which is roughly 240 to 250 mg of polyphenols per day.

Green and black tea come from the same plant. Black tea is made by letting the fresh tea leaves dry by exposure to air. This also causes fermentation which in turn produces oxidation. After air-drying for several hours, black-tea leaves are then cooked. By then, however, fermentation has destroyed most of the valuable anti-oxidants, or polyphenols, which are present in all fresh tea leaves. Fermentation produces the rich brown color preferred by some tea drinkers. In processing leaves for green tea, everything is done to prevent fermentation and oxidation. Green tea leaves are steamed immediately after picking—heat stops the fermentation process. Many types of Chinese tea, such as oolong, are partially fermented. They contain lower levels of polyphenols than green tea, but more than black tea.

Black tea contains the greatest amount of caffeine. Oolong has about half as much, and green tea has less than one-third the caffeine of black tea. Tea bags filled with tiny broken bits of tea leaves release twice as much caffeine as the equivalent amount of whole leaves. Green tea offers a stimulating pick-up without nervousness or sleepless nights.

TYPES OF JAPANESE GREEN TEA

Gyokuro is the most expensive and the best tea produced in Japan. When gyokuro is ground to a fine powder, it is called matcha or "liquid jade," and is used in the tea ceremony. Gyokuro and matcha account for less than one percent of the tea produced in Japan.

Sencha is the most popular kind of tea in Japan; it can vary greatly in price and quality. Bancha is the lowest grade of sencha and is made from large, coarse, older tea leaves. Because bancha contains less caffeine that other teas, it is sold in health food stores. Hōjicha results from roasted bancha leaves. Genmai cha is a mixture of bancha leaves and toasted, popped rice kernels—it is often called "popcorn tea."

Presentation, Presentation, Presentation

So much of what we enjoy about Japanese food is how it looks. If it looks great, it often tastes great. Japanese food is a sensory experience involving many of our senses. Here are some suggestions for making your dishes appeal to your visual sense.

CUTTING STYLES

RAN-GIRI (DIAGONAL CUT WHILE ROTATING)

TAZUNA (FOR KONNYAKU)

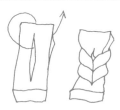

SEN-GIRI (JULIENNE)

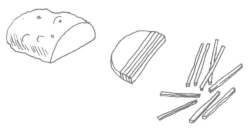

DISPLAY STYLES

RICE BALE STYLE (TAWARAMORI)   FLAT STYLE (HIRAMORI)

 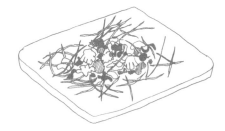

Excerpt from Chiura Obata: an Oral History

Courtesy of the University of California at Los Angeles Special Collections Library, Japanese American History Project

. . . There is something about Japanese food people don't talk about with western food; that is, Japanese cuisine respects quite strictly the season of the food: the different food for each season. . . .

When you say a different dish from the different seasons, for example, at the beginning of spring when the plum blossom starts to bloom, the buds start to release a mild and rich fragrance. You put that into your clear soup. If you hold your bowl, you see the seasonal fragrance of the plum. Of course, those kinds of Japanese bowls are highly sophisticated— they use the very valuable ones—so you enjoy the cuisine through the containers by great artists. It's a cuisine not only to taste and to enjoy with your mouth but also with your eyes. So, the other characteristic is that it has to be musical. There was this famous journalist, Marjorie Trumbull, who was writing a column for the *San Francisco Chronicle*, and she asked what we meant by this musical element. When I took her to a Japanese restaurant called Kikakku Restaurant I asked the hostess to serve kazunoko (herring roe) and kurage (jellyfish). As you know, when you bite kazunoko, in your mouth between your teeth it makes a small sound: pari, pari. As for kurage, it makes an even bigger sound. We associate this kind of sound to another (sound in nature). When you go to the mountains you learn the frog's cry—in one valley a small sound, in another valley a bigger sound, the sound of the rushing creek absorbs these—it's a type food value through the ears. These are aspects of Japanese cuisine. . . .

It is nice, on one hand, to have a huge steak which is enough for three persons, on a big western plate. But, after all, Japanese cuisine is a kind of sophisticated, unique culture, in which you enjoy each piece with its flavor, the container which complements the food, and the season.

NEW YEAR'S

In with the old . . . . in with the new.

OSHŌGATSU

Early immigrants to the United States valued the traditional customs and celebrations of their hometowns in Japan. Of the holidays that have survived through the generations, Oshōgatsu, or New Year's, holds a special place for Japanese Americans. Whether a family is Christian or Buddhist, Oshōgatsu remains a vital part of the traditions of every family of Japanese ancestry.

The word Oshōgatsu immediately brings mochi or pounded rice cakes to mind. At New Year's, mochi is served in a soup called Ozōni. Ozōni differs from region to region in Japan; the soup is seasoned differently from place to place and the ingredients may vary. For example, the most typical Osumashi, or soup, is made with konbu (dried kelp) or katsuo (shaved bonita flakes). In the Kyoto area, miso is the main ingredient in the soup. Besides the mochi, ingredients such as satoimo (taro), kamaboko (fishcake), mizuna (Japanese mustard greens), and spinach help make the soup colorful and add to the variety of flavors.

Many families continue the tradition of cleaning house, settling their debts, preparing special New Year's food called Osechi ryōri, and coming together as a family on New Year's Eve and New Year's Day. Families still visit friends and relatives on New Year's Day. Certain customs, such as giving Otoshidama (New Year's money), have been replaced by giving presents during Christmas. The custom of decorating the doorway with Kadomatsu (literally "door pine")— a symbolic decoration consisting of pine, bamboo and plum blossoms—is often replaced by a Christmas tree and its adornments.

Japanese American families still observe the decoration and display of the kagami mochi, a stack of large mochi decorated with konbu and an orange. To many, this display represents New Year's as much a decorated pine tree symbolizes Christmas. In recent years, Japanese American families living in urban areas can enjoy the traditional Kōhaku Utagassen (Red and White Song Contest) transmitted by satellite from Japan and broadcast on New Year's Eve. Some families eat toshikoshi soba (buckwheat noodles) on New Year's Eve.

On New Year's Day, many families begin by eating Ozōni (mochi soup) and the many Osechi dishes. Osechi ryōri traditionally consisted of vegetable dishes with ingredients representing symbols of good luck and fortune. Kuromame (black beans) symbolize good health, kobu/konbu (kelp) represents happiness because it appears in the word "yorokobu," and kazunoko (herring roe) is a symbol of many children.

As families have extended to the third, fourth or, in some cases, the fifth generation, a rich variety of food has appeared on the New Year's table. Besides the traditional Japanese New Year's dishes, other dishes representing American, Mexican, Hawai'ian, and other cuisines are eaten together for New Year's. This has created a truly international New Year's in Japanese American homes today.

—Norman Masuda

Basic Dashi for Soba or Ozōni

5 cups water
½ cup dried shrimp or 1 cup katsuobushi
5 inches dashi konbu

Wipe dashi konbu with a wet cloth and make a slit in the middle. Place konbu in a pot with cold water and cook over medium heat. Remove konbu when the water starts to boil. Add shrimp or katsuobushi, boil again, then remove from heat. Strain stock through a cheesecloth or a fine sieve. Broth should be clear.

Note: Some people add a sprinkle of sugar after second boil to enhance the flavor.

Ozōni (Mochi Soup)

5 cups dashi, simmering
½ teaspoon salt
1 teaspoon shōyu
1 carrot, thinly sliced
8 napa leaves, cut into 2-inch lengths
4 to 8 mochi

Bake mochi in 375 degree oven until it becomes a little soft, about five minutes. Place mochi in four bowls. Bring dashi to a boil. Add salt and shōyu to dashi. Cook carrot and napa in hot dashi for about five minutes. Pour over mochi in bowls. Serve immediately.

Fresh mochi is wonderful with the following: kinako flour mixed with a teaspoon of sugar and a sprinkle of salt; shōyu mixed with sugar; and just plain shōyu. Day old or frozen mochi is great toasted in the oven at 350 degrees until golden and puffy. Eat with shōyu and sugar.

Making a Wood Usu for Mochi

For those who have fantasies of pounding old fashioned mochi in a real wood usu (mortar), I made one recently and it's been so much fun using it! It brings back memories of Oshōgatsu in the Delta farms of California, where I grew up.

Rice, including mochigome (glutinous rice) was home grown. The rice was polished in a small machine then soaked in water and steamed in a piece of cloth in multi-tiered wood racks over an outdoor, wood-fired pot of boiling water. There was no particular rush to get to the pounding, for there was sake, beer, and finger food on hand. When my cousin announced the mochigome was done and the taste checked, the rice was dumped into the usu and the pounding began. The person in charge turned over the hot rice between the kine (pestle) beats until it became a smooth, glutinous mass. It was then brought indoors where the women had prepared tables covered with katakuriko (potato starch). One person would stretch out the whole batch and pinch off golf ball-sized pieces. She would pass it off to those around the table to mold into balls while still warm. They would then cool and harden them on plates or paper placed all about the room.

I would look for old usus in museums or people's homes. Unfortunately, many have disappeared and have been replaced with modern electrical machines—which make good mochi but certainly not like pounding your own. I decided to make my own usu for the Oshōgatsu Party that the Boston Japanese Oshōgatsu Group and Steve Nishino helped organize. Since my efforts turned out well, it is being shared as a "recipe" from New England.

I cut down an old oak tree which had its top blown off in a storm. I used the trunk of the tree about 20 feet from the base. It was about 20 inches in diameter, and I cut it into a length of 20 inches. I took my small 12 inch electric chain saw and started to gouge out a bowl shaped depression 12 inches in diameter. Since using the tip of the saw is not a recommended procedure, be very careful; do not push yourself.

The finished depression left a rim 2 to 4 inches. I chipped out the wood to a depth of 6 inches in the center, with a slightly dished bottom. The rough cut was made somewhat shallower, and the finishing was done with a heavy half-inch hand drill with a round

continued on next page

burr cutting tool to smooth out the rough finish. Finally, sanding disks were used to finish the bowl. I am sure there are easier ways to cut out the hollow, but this method was quite effective.

Handles were made with 8 inch tree branches attached with similar size wood spacers about one and a half inches at each end and secured with 6 inch tag bolts. These handles made it easy for two to carry the 128 pound usu. I finished the usu with several coats of satin varnish.

I made a kine from seasoned wood 2 inches in diameter and 11 inches long for the head, and a straight 40 inch branch about 1-1/4 inch in diameter for the handle. The thick end of the handle was cut to a rectangle. By drilling and filing the head, a matching rectangular hole was made to allow the handle to be attached. After a good fit was made, wood putty was used to fill in voids and a long screw through the head and handle secures the two pieces. This, too, was varnished.

To prevent scarring floors, a thick rug material was nailed onto the bottom of the usu. You have just made an usu!

POUNDING MOCHI

For two batches of mochi for the usu, wash and soak mochigome, sweet rice, in a large pot filled with water overnight. The next day, remove water and pour rice into cloth toweling and steam in the seiro, if available, or in an ordinary steamer. After a half hour or longer, sample the rice by biting into it. When it is adequately cooked, the kernels are uniformly soft and ready for pounding. The pounding process is vigorous and affords a good outlet for stored energy. A steady chant of, "Yoisho, yoisho, yoisho" by bystanders helps keep up the power and rhythm of the beat.

–Susumo Ito

Atsuyaki Tamago (Rolled Fried Egg)

3 large eggs
2 Tablespoons sugar
Pinch of salt
Pinch of ajinomoto, optional
¼ teaspoon of instant dashi
Vegetable oil (to coat frying pan)

Beat eggs well. Add seasonings. Stir to combine. Heat a large skillet or a Japanese square frying pan; brush with vegetable oil. Pour about ⅙ of the egg mixture into the pan. When this first layer is cooked, loosen the edges with a knife and, with a chopstick, roll the thin layer towards you. Each layer should be about ⅛ inch thick. Push the rolled egg to opposite end of the frying pan (away from you). Brush pan with vegetable oil. Pour another ⅙ of the egg mixture into the pan, making sure to lift the first rolled layer up so that the next layer of egg will coat the entire pan. When this layer is cooked, roll omelette toward you, making sure to fold first layer inside. Repeat process until egg mixture is used up. The finished rolled egg will be about 2 inches in diameter. Place egg on a sudare (bamboo sushi mat) and gently press to make it compact. Cut into horizontal slices to enjoy as an egg roll or slice into 4 to 5 pieces to use for makizushi.

Serves 4

Kabocha (Japanese Pumpkin)

1 kabocha or 2 acorn squash, cut into 1½ inch pieces

Sauce:
1 cup dashi
3 Tablespoons sugar
2 teaspoons shōyu
½ teaspoon salt

Wash kabocha. Cut in half. Scoop out seeds. Cut into 1½ inch pieces, leaving skin on but removing stem. Prepare sauce in a 3 quart pan. Combine sauce ingredients. Cook kabocha in sauce over low to medium heat until tender, about 20 to 30 minutes. Stir carefully and occasionally.

Serves 4 to 5

Kinpira Gobō (Stir-Fry Burdock)

3 or 4 stalks gobō (burdock root)
1 small round steak
1½ Tablespoon oil
½ teaspoon sugar
¼ teaspoon black pepper
3 Tablespoons shōyu
White sesame seeds, toasted, for garnish

Scrape skin off gobō with a knife or peeler. Shave or cut the gobō into thin strips. Soak in cold water. Slice steak into thin strips. Heat half of the oil in skillet and stir-fry the meat, sprinkling a little sugar over the meat as you stir-fry. Set aside. Drain the gobō and blot excess water with paper towels. Heat remaining oil in skillet and stir-fry gobō over medium high heat for 5 to 8 minutes. Add the meat and black pepper. Then add shōyu and stir until liquid is absorbed. Sprinkle with toasted sesame seeds before serving.

Serves 4 to 6

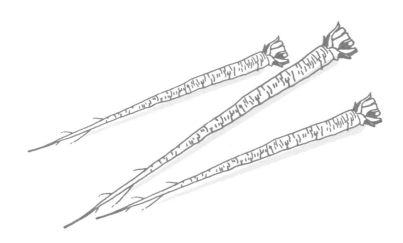

Food Symbolism

Mochi symbolizes longevity. Imo is believed to drive away evil spirits. Daikon and gobō mean a firm family foundation. Nori is auspicious. Eating ozōni as the first meal of the New Year is to hope that one's happy dreams are realized. Fish for New Year's is good luck. Kuromame signifies success and health. Renkon is, according to Buddhist tradition, a sacred plant. Dai dai, or a fruit with an orange color, is a wish for a long and prosperous life. Dried kaki signifies health and success in life.

Kinton (Mashed Sweet Potato and Chestnut)

- 1 pound sweet potato
- 1 Tablespoon white vinegar
- ¾ cup sugar
- 2 bottles of kuri (sweetened chestnut), reserve juice
- ⅓ cup kuri juice
- 1½ Tablespoons mirin

Peel the potatoes and cut into ¾ inch slices, then soak in water for 15 minutes. Drain and cover with water and 1 Tablespoon vinegar. Boil on high heat for 5 to 10 minutes. Drain, change water, bring to boil and cook for another 5 to 10 minutes. Drain, add water and 1 Tablespoon of sugar, and boil until soft. Taking one slice of potato at a time, press through a sieve with the back of a spoon while potato is hot. Combine the potato with the remaining sugar and ⅓ cup kuri juice in a pan and cook over high heat. Mix with a wooden paddle until it thickens and the paddle separates the potato in the pan. Add mirin to give lustre. Boil chestnuts in remaining syrup with a little water to soften the chestnuts. Add whole chestnuts to potato. Top potato with washed pine leaves for decoration.

Serves 4 to 6

Nimame

Born in the Meiji period in 1905, Kaoru Okawa Ito learned to cook at a young age. She recalls, "I was about seven years old in Yokohama, Japan, when my father, a merchant marine, returned from an overseas trip. He summoned me to buy some assorted Japanese cooked vegetables for nishime. I wanted so badly to impress him, but I was too embarrassed to ask him what it was. I thought that he said oshime, which was diaper. With money in hand, I trotted off to the store to buy something to eat. I had a chance to buy my favorite food, nimame (cooked sweet beans). There were all kinds of beans; they were the cheapest food staple in those days, and cost only about 2 yen. I bought all kinds of nimame and brought them home, proud of my haul. My father saw what I had brought and reprimanded me, saying, 'Don't you know what nishime is? From here on, you must learn whatever you can about Japanese cuisine.'"

Nimame (Sweet Beans)

      1 cup pink beans
      2 cups (approximately) water
      ½ cup sugar
      1 teaspoon salt
      2 Tablespoons white vinegar

Place beans in pan. Cover with 2 inches of water. Soak overnight. Do not drain. On stovetop, at medium heat, bring to a boil. Remove awae (foamy residue). Replace water with 1 inch fresh water. After 1 to 1½ hours of boiling beans, taste and check for doneness and consistency.

Add sugar, salt, and vinegar. Add more sugar and salt to taste if needed.

Ohagi (Mochi Rice Ball)

> 1½ cups fresh azuki beans
>
> 1½ cups sugar
>
> ¼ to ½ teaspoon salt
>
> 3 cups sweet rice (using cup from rice cooker or 2⅓ cups with standard cup)

To prepare an, add water to azuki beans and soak overnight. Add more water, if necessary, and bring to a boil, stirring periodically to prevent burning, cooking slowly until done. Drain liquid until there is just enough to blend easily. Put in blender and blend until smooth. Return to pot. Stir in sugar and salt. Cook down the liquid on medium heat, stirring constantly (be careful of the hot splatters), until it is the right consistency for spreading on the rice balls. Cool and refrigerate overnight if desired.

Rinse rice until fairly clean and not cloudy. Pour in rice cooker, then add equal amount of water as rice. Do not soak the rice and cook right away. Add a sprinkle of salt to prevent cooked rice from getting hard. Note—the cooked rice is very sticky.

To make ohagi, wet palms and fingers with water before forming balls of rice (about 18 large or 36 small). Place the rice balls on moistened dinner plates to prevent them from sticking. Moisten left hand and place a teaspoon of an on it. Form into a flat patty. Place the ball of rice in the middle of the an. With moistened fingers, pull up and smooth the an around the rice ball. Place each on individual cupcake liners if desired.

The completed ohagi does not freeze well; however, the an can be frozen ahead of time.

Su Renkon (Lotus Root Salad)

  1 piece renkon (lotus root), about 10 inches long

⅛ cup dried shrimp, chopped

¼ cup rice vinegar

  2 Tablespoons water

  2 Tablespoons sugar

     Pinch of salt

  1 Tablespoon fresh ginger, slivered

¼ cup kamaboko, slivered

Peel renkon and thinly slice crosswise. Bring a pot of water to boil. Add renkon and cook just until renkon is clear and transparent. Do not overcook. Remove from heat, drain, and cool. Make sauce by combining chopped dried shrimp, vinegar, water, and sugar. Add renkon and toss. Last, add ginger and kamaboko. Refrigerate.

Serves 4 to 6

OKINAWAN AMERICAN NEW YEAR'S CUSTOMS AND CELEBRATIONS

Traditionally, Okinawan Americans have benefited from cultural influences from both China and Japan in celebrating the New Year. Thus, both the solar and lunar New Year's have played prominent roles in the lives of Americans of Okinawan descent.

In Okinawa, the Lunar New Year is a three-day holiday starting on the first day of the first lunar month. As in China and Japan, preparations are made for the New Year by cleaning house, taking baths, and paying off old debts. During the 12th month, the New Year pig is slaughtered for use in preparing the New Year's dishes.

An important custom is to start the New Year with new water (wakamiji, or "young water"). New water is taken from a well or spring to be placed on the ancestral altar (tōtōme) or on the shelf of the "fire god" (Fii nu Kan) in the kitchen. The first tea of the New Year is made with this "young water."

The New Year is a time for visiting village shrines, temples, and sacred places. People visit relatives and hold family reunions.

As part of the New Year's celebrations, decorations are placed in appropriate locations: young pine is offered to the fire god and a decoration consisting of rice cakes, kelp, charcoal, and oranges is arranged in the alcove (Tukunumē = Tokonoma in Japanese) or the ancestral altar. These represent the riches of the field, the sea, and the mountains.

There is an Okinawan poem for the New Year's:

> *Aratama nu tushi ni, tan tu kubu kazati, kukuru kara sigata, wakaku nayusa.*
> "For New Year's charcoal and kelp is decorated, from our hearts to our whole appearance, there is a feeling of renewed youthfulness."

The families get together, feast on delicacies prepared and served in laquerware boxes (Tundaabun), drink sake or awamori (distilled liquor), and sing to music played on the Sanshin (Okinawan samisen).

In overseas communities of Okinawan Americans, some of the same foods are prepared for New Year's, either solar or lunar, but Japanese and other dishes are added to the feast.

—NORMAN MASUDA

Kufa Jūshii (Okinawan Pilaf)

      3 cups rice, washed and drained
   3¼ cups pork stock
      ½ pound pork (belly pork), boiled, cooled, and diced
      3 medium shiitake, soaked, drained, and diced
      1 medium carrot, diced
      1 block kamaboko, diced
      ¼ cup green peas, parboiled and drained
      2 Tablespoons oil
      1 Tablespoon salt
      ½ Tablespoon shōyu

Wash rice, drain, and set aside for 2 to 3 hours. Boil pork, let cool, then dice. Dice shiitake mushrooms, carrots, and kamaboko. Parboil peas, drain. Sauté rice in oil until golden brown; add pork, shiitake, carrots, pork stock, salt, and shōyu and mix thoroughly. Cover and steam for 10 minutes over low heat. Add green peas and kamaboko, mix, and continue to steam until rice is cooked.

Serves 5

Rafute (Glazed Pork)

      3 pounds pork (belly pork), boiled, cooled and cut into 1½ inch cubes
      1 cup pork stock (left over from boiling pork)
      ½ cup sugar
      1 cup shōyu
      1 cup awamori, whiskey, or sake
      1 inch piece of ginger, minced
      1 clove garlic, minced
      ½ cup mirin

Boil pork for 40 minutes. Cool pork and save stock. Cut pork into 1½ inch cubes. In pot, add pork and pork stock, then bring to a boil. Add sugar, ½ cup shōyu, awamori, ginger, and garlic. Cover and simmer over medium heat for 30 minutes. Add ½ cup shōyu and ½ cup mirin, and simmer uncovered for 1½ hours. Turn occasionally until meat is glazed and tender.

Note: When reheating pork, add a little sake or pork stock.

Ashi Tibichi (Pig's Feet Soup)

  4 pounds pig's feet

  3 strips nishime konbu

  3 medium daikon (or carrots or gobō)

10 cups konbu soaking liquid

  1 package dashi or 2 teaspoons instant dashi

  2 Tablespoons salt

¼ cup shōyu

  1 Tablespoon grated ginger

   Okinawan pepper, or pepper, or shichimi

Singe and broil pig's feet until brown and burnt. Rinse under warm water, scraping off charred areas. Cut into 3 inch pieces. Put into large pot, add 2 quarts water, and bring to boil. Simmer for 10 minutes, then remove feet and drain. Wash konbu and soak for ½ hour in 10 cups of water. Tie into knots and cut between knots. Set aside. Peel and cut daikon (or other vegetables) into 2 inch lengths. Put 10 cups of konbu soaking liquid into pot, add feet, and simmer for 1 hour. Add daikon and instant dashi and simmer for ½ hour or until daikon is cooked. Add konbu. Add salt and shōyu and set aside for 4 to 5 hours for flavor to soak in. Reheat and serve with grated ginger and pepper.

Serves 8

My Memories of New Year's

Steven Oshiro remembers growing up on Oahu and celebrating New Year's: "Although I've been living on the Mainland for 18 years, I still have fond memories of growing up in Hawai'i. I especially remember all the 'good eats' while growing up. I always looked forward to New Year's when my mother would spend hours working on the New Year's food. She would make the traditional futomaki, sashimi, namasu, shrimp tenpura, pig's feet soup, andagii, but my favorite would be the kūbu iricha. I remember the konbu, konnyaku, buta (pork), and the kamaboko all mixed and cooked together. This savory dish served with rice truly 'broke the mouth'."

Kūbu Irichi (Also called Kūbu Iricha) (Sautéed Kelp and Vegetables)

    1 package (1½ ounce size) nishime konbu (dried kelp strips)
    ½ pound belly pork, boiled or cooked 30 minutes
    1 block konnyaku
    6 dried shiitake, soaked in water
    3 age dōfu, cut in thin strips
    1 block kamaboko
    2 Tablespoons salad oil
    3 cups pork stock
    ¼ cup shōyu
    3 Tablespoons sake
    2 Tablespoons mirin
    2 Tablespoons sugar
 1½ teaspoon salt
    1 Tablespoon dashi no moto

Add nishime konbu to boiling water and boil for 10 minutes. Cool and cut into thin strips. Boil pork for 30 minutes or until done, and cut into thin strips. Save pork stock. Cut konnyaku into thin strips, parboil, and cool. Add age dōfu to boiling water to remove oil, drain, and cut into thin strips. Soak shiitake in water for 20 minutes and cut into thin strips. Cut kamaboko into thin strips. Heat oil in pan and add konnyaku, shiitake, age dōfu, pork, and konbu. Sauté for a few minutes. Add pork stock, dashi no moto, shōyu, sake, mirin, sugar and salt. Cook over low heat for 1 hour until konbu gets soft. Finally, add kamaboko and cook for 5 more minutes.

Serves 8

Sōkibuni (Spare Rib Soup)

- 1 pound spare ribs, cut into 1½ inch lengths
- 4 cups water
- 2 cups dashi
- 1 package nishime konbu (dried kelp strips), tied into knots 1½ inches long
- 1 medium daikon, peeled and sliced into ½ inch pieces
- 6 medium shiitake, soaked and cut into ½ inch lengths, stems removed
- ½ pound mustard cabbage, parboiled
- 2 teaspoons salt
- 1 teaspoon shōyu

Wash konbu, tie into knots, and cut between the knots. Remove stems from shiitake mushrooms and cut into ½ inch lengths. Parboil mustard cabbage, drain, and cut into 1½ inch lengths. Peel and slice daikon into ½ inch pieces. Put spare ribs, konbu, daikon, and shiitake in pot with 4 cups water.

Simmer over medium heat for 1 hour. When spare ribs are soft, remove ribs and vegetables and set aside. Strain liquid. Put strained stock into pot, add 2 cups dashi, and bring to boil. Add salt and shōyu; adjust seasoning. Add mustard cabbage before serving.

Serves 5

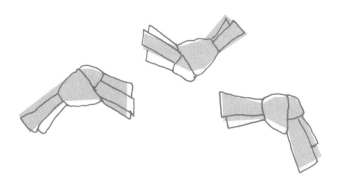

Food and the Okinawan Experience

In late summer of every year, the Hawai'i United Okinawa Association hosts an Okinawan Festival at Kapiolani Park near Waikiki. Thousands of people attend this fun, three-day event. My husband and I participate as often as we can because we enjoy the camaraderie of our Ginoza Sonjin Kai, and always come away energized by being a part of something larger than ourselves.

One year I was asked to make andagii (round Okinawan donuts) dough for the festival. The dough would be made in a large commercial kitchen then carted to the park and fried in large woks under the tents. The sweet smell of frying andagii usually draws large crowds, so the dough for this very popular donut must be carefully prepared and mixed in large vats. The issei and nisei women strictly and precisely instruct and oversee the making of the dough. As a sansei, I was told exactly how and when to add the ingredients, how much pressure to apply to the dough as the wet ingredients were mixed with the dry, and how to use my arms to carefully fold the dough. And, of course, never—ever—overmix the batter.

After several scoldings and several successful batches of dough, I was told I could wash up and rest. I was pleased and proud of myself for earning the praise of the issei women. As I washed my arms, I happily reflected on the wonderful donuts we created. But soon these warm feelings turned into panic when I couldn't wash the dough off my arms! The sticky dough had rolled into little balls and tangled itself into the hair on my arms! I couldn't get it off! It took several days of scrubbing, rubbing, and picking at the dough before all the balls were dislodged. After this ordeal, I had to laugh—what a way to be reminded of my Okinawan heritage.

–Ann S. Yabusaki

Satā Andagii (Okinawan Doughnuts)

- 4 cups flour
- 4 teaspoons baking powder
- 2 cups sugar
- 4 eggs
- 1 teaspoon vanilla extract
- 1 6-ounce carton of whipping cream
  Grated orange peel, optional
  Sesame seeds, optional
- 1 package barbecue sticks

Sift flour and baking powder together and set aside. Beat eggs, then add sugar, whipping cream, and vanilla. Add dry ingredients gradually to egg mixture. Mix but don't overmix. Drop by spoonfuls into 375 degree oil. Fry until golden brown. Drain on paper towels. Balls may be rolled in grated orange peel or sesame seeds. Put 3 to 5 balls on a barbecue stick. Serve while still warm.

You may drop dough Okinawan style into the hot oil. Fill right palm with dough. Lift and turn palm downwards, squeezing dough towards thumb, shaping into a round ball. Move right thumb over index finger and gently drop dough into hot oil.

NEW TRADITIONS

Family New Year

On New Year's Day for many years, I used to get up at 4:00 a.m. and make norimaki and inarizushi before attending with my grandchildren the 10:00 a.m. "Shūshō-e" Service at the Buddhist Church. After returning home from the service, I would then prepare the ozōni and, with my daughter and grandchildren, would partake of our usual New Year's breakfast of ozōni (mochi soup), kuromame (black beans), kuri (chestnut), and mikan (Japanese orange). I would have prepared the other foods for New Year's the day before, which resulted in all day cooking. Now that I am growing older, as are the grandchildren, I am able to get up leisurely on New Year's. After the church service and the first meal for the year, my daughter and grandchildren make the sushi and the various other dishes, before the other members of the family join us to celebrate the New Year. Among the 15 or more different dishes we prepare for the New Year feast, Sweet and Sour Chicken Drummettes is a favorite.

–IRENE SAIKI

Sweet and Sour Chicken Drummettes

    2 packages (24) drummettes
      Cornstarch
    2 eggs, slightly beaten with 1 Tablespoon water
      Oil for frying, just enough to brown drummettes
    1 cup sugar
    ½ cup white vinegar
    ¼ cup water
    3 Tablespoons catsup
    2 Tablespoons shōyu
    ½ teaspoon salt

Preheat oven to 350 degrees. Heat oil in skillet. Roll drummettes in cornstarch. Dip in beaten eggs with a little water added. Brown drummettes on both sides in oil. Line the browned drummettes in baking dish. Mix together remaining ingredients for sauce. Pour sauce over the drummettes. Bake in oven for 25 to 30 minutes, turning chicken after the first 15 minutes.

This is a potluck favorite of our family, especially for the New Year dessert tray. It's a Hawai'ian innovation of the traditional Japanese gelatin, called kanten. It is as pretty and festive as it is light and delicious.

– YOSHIE IWAHASHI

Foamy Three-Layered Coconut Kanten

1 stick red kanten (agar agar stick)

1 stick white kanten

3 cups water

1 cup sugar

1 12-ounce can of coconut milk, thawed if frozen

2 egg whites

1 teaspoon lemon juice or white vinegar

Tear kanten sticks into small bits; soak in water for ½ hour. Cook kanten mixture over medium heat until it boils and kanten is melted. Add sugar and cook for 1 minute. Add coconut milk and cook mixture for few minutes. Beat egg whites with lemon juice until stiff but not dry. Pour about 1½ cups of kanten mixture through sieve and set aside. Pour remaining mixture through sieve directly into 8-inch square glass cake pan; set aside.

To prepare the foamy layer, pour reserved 1½ cups kanten mixture into beaten egg whites and fold. Slowly pour over hot layer in pan. Cool to room temperature and then chill until it jells. Cut into desired shapes. It is especially pretty when cut into thin rectangles with a corrugated kanten knife.

Hapa New Year

My husband, who is part Finnish, makes this Scandinavian specialty, which is a type of pickled salmon. Given the mixed (and mixed-up) nature of our household, items that started out with one purpose sometimes find another. In this case, my husband found that the screw-down type of tsukemono press made the perfect implement for marinating the salmon. He now brings this dish to my mother's house for Oshōgatsu.

–Pat Abe-Calef

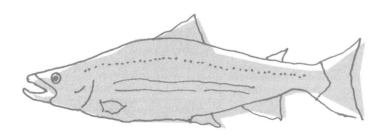

Gravlax

2 pounds boneless salmon pieces or fillets, skin attached

1 small bunch fresh baby dill weed

1 teaspoon dill seed

2 Tablespoons coarse salt (kosher salt works well and is inexpensive)

4 Tablespoons sugar

¼ teaspoons freshly ground pepper

¼ teaspoons ground allspice

¼ to ⅓ cup Aquavit (a Danish liquor)

Mustard Dill Sauce:

¼ cup Dijon mustard

1 teaspoon dry mustard

3 Tablespoons sugar

2 Tablespoons white wine vinegar

⅓ cup olive oil

¼ cup fresh baby dill weed, chopped

With a knife, score skin side of salmon in several places. Mix together the dill weed and dill seed; rub mixture on both sides of salmon. Mix together salt, sugar, pepper, and allspice; rub over salmon, patting lightly into the flesh. Place salmon at bottom of tsukemono press, skin side down. Pour Aquavit over fish. Screw down press so that some liquid oozes around the edges, but not so hard that the fish is squashed. Refrigerate for two to three days. From time to time, release press and spoon juices over fish. Screw back down, keeping skin side down.

To serve, thinly slice across the grain on a diagonal, cutting the flesh away from the skin. Serve with Mustard Dill Sauce on cocktail rye bread or sturdy crackers.

Mustard Dill Sauce:

In a food processor or whisking briskly, mix together the mustards, sugar, and vinegar. Slowly drizzle in the olive oil while machine is running or while whisking, until the mixture is the thickness of a light mayonnaise. Stir in the baby dill weed.

New Year's Celebration at the Kekaha Sugar Plantation

According to my dad, Kauai was the ideal place to grow up. Some of his favorite childhood remembrances are the New Year's celebrations that his family had in Kekaha.

His "Baba-chan's" (Grandma's) house, on the Kekaha Sugar Plantation, was the center of activity. About 2 days before New Year's, aunts, uncles, and cousins would gather at the house for mochi-tsuki. The women cooked the rice and the men took turns pounding it until it was smooth and sticky, ready to be made into rice cakes and mochi.

First, the living room was cleaned and low tables were set along the center of the room. Then, 4 to 5 hibachis were set in a row on the tables for the big Hekka (Sukiyaki) contest. His mother and Baba-chan would prepare all of the vegetables and chicken, and set them out next to the hibachis. In addition to the hekka, there was rice, makizushi (with unagi), sliced fruit, vegetable relishes, and kuromame. And, plenty of dried ika was on hand to munch on all day long.

Around 5:00 p.m., all of the relatives would arrive from around the island—Waimea, Hanapepe, etc. Each of the men chose a hibachi, and the contest was on to see who could make the tastiest Chicken Hekka! According to my dad, his father's Hekka usually won first place; he says the secret was using a lot of butter to give it that special ono (Hawai'ian for "good") flavor!

Plenty of beer (for the adults) and soda pop (for the kids) was served along with the Hekka and, after stuffing themselves for the first round, the men would fall asleep for a few hours while the kids ran around the house and yard making trouble. Around 10 p.m., the men would wake up and eat some more! Of course, even after all this feasting, there was always room for dessert—kanten, yōkan, and mochi.

Then, Uncle Charlie, the family musician and comedian extraordinaire, would entertain everyone with jokes, music, and magic tricks. He could play the ukulele and sing better than anyone else. And, he could wiggle his ears on command!

Then, at midnight—the main fireworks festivities began! Two long strings of firecrackers were hung from the Norfolk pine trees in front of the house. At midnight, they were lit and boy, were they loud! The boys, including my dad, got to play with sparklers, firecrackers, and (the now illegal) Roman Candles. On New Year's Day, the family would visit others on the plantation and share plates of fresh Hekka and mochi. Of course, the men were a bit preoccupied with the most ancient ritual of all . . . Bowl Games! They would listen to the Rose, Cotton, and Sugar Bowl games on the radio all day long. Some traditions never change!

–Jennifer Matsumura

Chicken Hekka

      2 Tablespoons butter
1 to ½ pounds chicken, sliced thinly
      1 cup shōyu, divided
      ½ cup sugar, divided
      1 can mushrooms, sliced
      1 can bamboo shoots, sliced thinly
      1 bundle long rice (bean thread), soaked in water until soft
      1 cup chicken broth or water
      ½ pounds watercress, optional
      1 bunch green onions, cut in 1½ inch lengths
         Dash of sake

Heat butter in large skillet. Brown ⅓ of the chicken, then add ⅓ cup shōyu and 2 Tablespoons sugar. Cook for a few minutes. Add ⅓ of the mushrooms, bamboo shoots, long rice, and chicken stock, and cook for 3 to 4 more minutes. Add ⅓ of the watercress and green onions. Add more shōyu, sugar, and water if necessary. Add sake. Serve immediately with hot rice. Prepare more hekka in batches with remaining ingredients.

Nishime (Simmered Pork with Vegetables)

  2 strips nishime konbu

  3 pieces dried shiitake, soaked, washed, and cut into 1 inch pieces

  ½ pound pork, cut into bite-size

  2 Tablespoons oil

  3 aburage, sliced

1½ cups water

  2 konnyaku, sliced into 1½ inch rectangles

  1 cup daikon, cut into 1½ inch pieces

  1 cup bamboo shoots, cut into 1½ inch pieces

  2 cups araimo, peeled and cut into 1½ inch pieces

  1 cup carrots, peeled and sliced into 1½ inch pieces

  1 cup gobō, peeled and cut into ¼ inch thick diagonal slices
    and soaked in water until used

  ½ cup shōyu

  ⅓ cup sugar

Soak konbu and shiitake in water for 10 minutes or until soft. Wash and strip konbu down center lengthwise, if more than 3 inches wide. Tie in knots, about 2 inches apart. Cut between the knots. Fry pork in oil until light brown. Add water, mushrooms, aburage, and konbu. Cover and cook for 10 minutes. Next, add konnyaku, daikon, carrots, and gobō. Stir and let cook for 15 minutes. Add seasonings and cook for 5 more minutes. Last, add araimo and bamboo shoots and cook until done, about 15 minutes.

My mother Matsy, created this dish after noticing how good other raw seafood dishes, such as namako, tasted when mixed with shredded daikon. She experimented until she came up with this recipe. Many oyster lovers enjoy this dish. We have shared this dish during Oshōgatsu for many years.

– SANDY INABA

Fresh Oysters with Shredded Radish (Daikon)

  2 10-ounce jars small oysters, cut into smaller pieces
  1 cup shredded daikon
  ½ lemon, quartered and sliced
     Juice from 1½ lemons
  1 Tablespoon parsley, finely chopped
  2 Tablespoons rice vinegar
1½ Tablespoons sugar (to enhance)
  1 teaspoon ajinomoto, optional

Rinse oysters and strain. Turn into glass bowl. Add rest of ingredients and mix well. Keep cold.

Satoimo (Simmered Taro)

6 to 10 satoimo (depending on size)

    Breast and thigh of one chicken

2½ cups dashi

3 Tablespoons sugar

1 teaspoon salt

3 Tablespoons sake

3 Tablespoons shōyu

Wash and peel the satoimo. Soak in water for about 15 minutes, then wash satoimo with salt to remove stickiness. Do not cut up satoimo; they should be cooked whole. Cut chicken into bite-size pieces.

Mix sugar, salt, and sake into the dashi and start cooking the satoimo over slow heat. Be sure to use otoshibuta (lid). After 20 minutes, add chicken and shōyu. Cook for an additional 10 minutes on low heat, until satoimo is tender. Remove from heat and let sit for 20 to 30 minutes. This way, the sauce will soak into the satoimo. This is ideal for a picnic bentō, too. You can also add takenoko, chicken, or jagaimo (potato).

Peanut Butter Shira-ae (Peanut Butter Vegetable Tōfu)

1 Tablespoon peanut butter

2 Tablespoons sugar

3 Tablespoons miso

½ block tōfu

    Juice from ½ of a lemon

2 cups napa cabbage

1½ cups broccoli, cooked

1½ cups celery, sliced very thin, rubbed with salt, and refreshed in cold water

Rinse tōfu. Squeeze dry in clean dish towel. Place tōfu with peanut butter, sugar, miso, and lemon juice in a suribachi or bowl to blend. Add suggested vegetables or abalone to this mixture. Mix thoroughly but carefully.

Additions:

Spinach, cucumbers (seeded, thinly sliced, and rubbed with salt), cooked green beans, thinly sliced abalone for garnish

Umani (Stewed Chicken with Vegetables)

2 chicken breasts

1 Tablespoon oil

4 shiitake

4 satoimo

2 gobō stalks

3 carrots

1 medium can bamboo shoots

1 block konnyaku

1 chikuwa (broiled fish cake)

1½ cups dashi

2 Tablespoons shōyu

1 teaspoon sugar

Soften shiitake in lukewarm water; drain and cut into quarters. Peel skin of satoimo and cut into wedges. Scrape off skin from gobō and cut into 1 inch lengths. Slice the remaining ingredients into bite-size pieces. Cut chicken into bite-size pieces. Heat oil in a skillet and stir-fry chicken until golden brown. Add shiitake, satoimo, gobō, carrots, bamboo shoots, and konnyaku and cook for 5 minutes. Add chikuwa, dashi, shōyu, and sugar and simmer for about 15 minutes, stirring occasionally. Serve hot or cold.

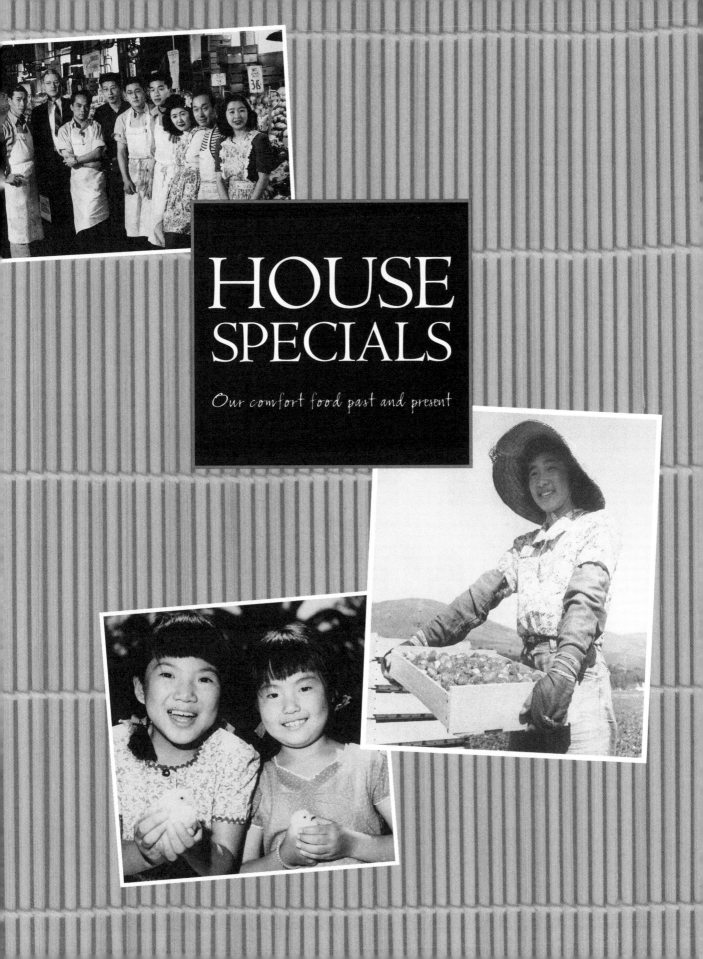

HOUSE SPECIALS

Our comfort food past and present

GOHAN SPECIAL

Raising Rice Consciousness

I grew up in Hawai'i where rice is a daily fact of life. Nori musubi is a picnic treat. Plate lunches have two scoops of rice with everything. You grow up hearing, "We were so poor we only had rice and kōko (pickles) to eat. . . ." Making rice was one of my the first jobs in the kitchen. Now I am raising two boys on the mainland, and I worry about them not sharing the Hawai'i side of their heritage.

We had just returned from a two week trip on the East Coast. Sitting at the table to a homecooked dinner, my son announced he missed rice. I guess I don't have to worry after all!

–GAYLE T. NISHIKAWA

Sushi Gohan

Per three cups uncooked rice:
- ¾ cup rice vinegar
- ¾ cup sugar
- 1 teaspoon salt

Warm vinegar, sugar and salt in pan over low heat until sugar is dissolved. Pour over hot, cooked rice; toss and mix thoroughly. For a shiny appearance, briskly fan rice while mixing. Use this recipe for making sushi.

Layered Rice

  1 1.5-ounce package nori goma furikake
  1 1.7-ounce package shiofuku konbu
  ½ cup chopped takuan or sanbaizuke
  4 cups cooked rice

Lay waxed paper on a 9 x 13 inch pan. Sprinkle nori goma furikake evenly on the wax paper. Sprinkle shiofuku konbu evenly over furikake. Do not use the salt that settles on the bottom of the package. Lay half of the cooked rice on the konbu. Press down with a moistened shamoji (rice paddle). Lay chopped takuan on the rice layer. Put the rest of the rice over the takuan and press down firmly. Let the rice set for an hour. Turn the pan upside down over a flat rectangular dish. Cut into squares and serve.

You can add more color to the dish by sprinkling the top with shredded red ginger, slivered pink kamaboko, or more toasted goma sprinkled over the top.

California Roll Cake

4 to 5 cups rice, cooked
      Sushi Gohan vinegar sauce
    8 packages seasoned nori strips
2 to 3 avocados
    1 package imitation crab meat, shredded
1 to 2 cucumbers, chopped
      Mayonnaise
      Goma nori furikake

Prepare 4 to 5 cups of rice and season with vinegar sauce. Layer half the rice in a flat 9 x 13 inch pan. Tear 4 packages of seasoned nori strips into pieces. Layer on top of rice. Slice 2 to 3 avocados and layer avocado slices with thin layer of mayonnaise on top of rice/nori layer. Mix together 1 package of crabmeat and chopped cucumber with mayonnaise and put on top of avocado layer. Tear remaining 4 packages of nori into pieces. Layer on top of crab mixture. Layer rest of rice on top. Garnish with goma nori furikake.

Barazushi

    5 cups rice, washed
    ½ cup white vinegar
    ½ cup sugar
    2 teaspoons salt
    4 age
    5 large shiitake, soaked in warm water
    ⅓ small package kanpyō, soaked
    4 cups water
    2 teaspoons salt
    4 Tablespoons sugar
    2 Tablespoons shōyu
    1 Tablespoon mirin
    1 large or 2 small gobō
    2 carrots
10 to 15 green beans

Garnish:
    3 eggs
    1 Tablespoon sugar
    ½ teaspoon salt
    1 can tuna
      Red food coloring
      Sugar and salt to taste
    1 sheet sushi nori

Cook rice in usual manner. Heat vinegar, sugar, and salt in small pan until dissolved. Cool. Put cooked rice in a large bowl. Sprinkle with vinegar mixture gradually. Mix well with a shamoji to cool rice.

Boil age for 15 minutes in 2 cups water. Squeeze all water from age and discard liquid. Combine water, salt, sugar, shōyu, and mirin in pan. Add boiled age, shiitake, and kanpyō and cook for 45 minutes. Drain the vegetables, saving the liquid for gobō. When cool, chop very fine and set aside. Scrape gobō and cut into very thin strips. Cook in saved liquid for 20 minutes. Set aside. Cut carrots and green beans in slivers and finely chop. Cover with water, season with salt, and cook until tender. Drain and set aside. Add cooked vegetables to the rice mixture. Mix throughly. Serve in bowl or platter.

Garnish:

Beat eggs, sugar, and salt together with fork or chopsticks until well blended. Fry in thin sheets. Repeat until all egg batter is used. Cut into 1 inch strips, and then crosswise into very thin strips. Drain tuna and crumble in a clean towel, then rinse in water to remove oil and fishy smell. Add 3 drops red food coloring and mix until color is well blended, then squeeze until dry. Mix tuna with a little sugar and salt, then place in frying pan and cook over low heat until well blended and dry. Toast nori in dry skillet and crush. Sprinkle eggs, tuna, and nori over the rice mixture. Pickled sliced ginger can also be a garnish.

Red Copper Salmon Sushi

Rice:

    3 cup rice

    3 cups water

    2 Tablespoons sake

    1 5-inch dashi konbu, optional, to place over rice

4 to 5 shiitake, soaked in warm water

      Shōyu and sugar to taste

    ½ pound salmon

    ⅛ pound (or 2-ounces) green colored tsukemono, chopped

    2 Tablespoons sesame seeds, toasted

Vinegar Sauce:

    5 Tablespoons vinegar

2 to 3 Tablespoons sugar

    1½ teaspoon salt

Optional Garnish: fine, sliced egg, sliced nori

Wash rice and before cooking, add water, sake, and konbu. Flake salmon meat that has been steamed, baked or grilled. Remove bones. Mix vinegar sauce ingredients into a small sauce pan and cook until sugar dissolves. Cool. Toss and mix well, cooled vinegar sauce into rice. Slice softened shiitake and sauté in shōyu and sugar. Combine salmon, tsukemono, seeds, and shiitake and add to rice. Mix well. Garnish with finely sliced egg and sliced yaki nori.

Onigiri

Masa Satow provides some helpful hints on our favorite dish.

I always add salt to the rice before cooking it. It eliminates salting just the outside of onigiri and it tastes better. Keep a bowl of salted water to dip your hands in. However if you make the onigiri using plastic wrap, you do not need to wet your hands. Put some rice in the center of a square piece (5 to 6 inches) of plastic wrap. Place umeboshi or other favorite filling on center top of rice. Close the wrap completely and twist the ends. Shape into triangle shape by molding with two hands. When I make ohagi, I use a double layer of plastic wrap. Dip in water once and use the same method as above. It's easier than using 2 layers of damp cheese cloth.

I like umeboshi, but my daughters prefer canned tuna no iritsuke. Place one small 3 ounce can of oil or waterpacked tuna. (I like the oiled tuna better.)

Put into a small skillet. Add shōyu, and a little ajinomoto to taste. Add around 2 teaspoons sugar, to taste. Do not make it too dry. I put one heaping teaspoon on each onigiri. Sprinkle toasted sesame seeds or shiso no furikake, or wrap in nori. Nori wilts easily so I place the nori on a plate and leave it for people to wrap their own. You can also gently mix in the furikake with a fork into the rice.

The following are the salt proportions: For 4 Japanese cups of rice (3 American cups) 1-3/4 teaspoon salt. For 5 Japanese cups (3-3/4 American cups) 2-1/4 teaspoon salt.

Did you know umeboshi keeps the rice from spoiling?

Chirashizushi

6 cups sushi gohan

2 medium carrots, cut into small cubes or slivers

3 Tablespoons water

2 Tablespoons sugar

½ teaspoon shōyu

15 string beans, cut into slivers

1 Tablespoon water

1 Tablespoon sugar

⅛ teaspoon salt

8 medium dried shiitake, soaked in warm water and cut into small pieces

4 Tablespoons water

3 Tablespoons sugar

1 Tablespoon shōyu

Add first four ingredients and cook on high heat until liquid evaporates. Stir constantly. Set aside. Repeat with next four ingredients. Repeat again with last four ingredients. Add the above to sushi gohan using 6 cups of cooked rice. To garnish use toasted nori slivers or benishōga. Fried egg strips can also be used.

Fried egg strips:

3 eggs

1 Tablespoon cornstarch

2 Tablespoons water

½ teaspoon salt

1 teaspoon sugar

Oil for frying

Beat eggs. Mix cornstarch and water first before adding to egg. Add salt and sugar and beat again. Fry a thin layer of egg in a lightly oiled pan. Carefully lift all edges and flip egg over. Turn over on to paper towel and let slightly cool. Cut into thin strips. Repeat cooking steps until egg is all used.

Mama Nakano

This dish came with my mother-in-law to this country in the 1920s. Its ingredients reflect the dish's origins in Japanese rural life. Like most issei women, she didn't have a recipe and tended to use whatever ingredients she had on hand. The results were somewhat mixed.

That's not to say you can't vary the ingredients. A couple of times, when I received some matsutake from a friend, for instance, I substituted it for the shiitake, leaving out the gobō, so that the taste of the coveted mushroom comes through.

I usually serve the aji gohan with spinach shira-ae, or other vegetables and tōfu, for added protein and for a complete meal. Aji Gohan isn't particularly elegant and it isn't hard to make. But as my husband says, "It's really good."

– Mei Nakano

Mama Nakano's Aji Gohan

  1 large carrot, peeled

½ gobō, about 12 inches long, peeled

  1 cup bamboo shoots, fresh or canned

  5 medium dried shiitake

  2 boneless, skinless chicken breasts

  1 teaspoon oil

  4 cups non-fat chicken broth with 2 teaspoons instant dashi added

  1 Tablespoon mirin

  3 Tablespoons shōyu

½ teaspoon salt

  1 Tablespoon sugar

  2 cups rice

  1 cup frozen peas

Soak dried shiitake in warm water for one hour. Slice thin, then across in 1 inch pieces. Slice carrots, gobō, and bamboo shoots into 1 inch long julienne sticks. Cut chicken into ½ inch cubes.

Lightly sauté chicken in oil in stew pot. Add carrots, gobō, bamboo shoots, and shiitake and continue cooking for one minute. Add chicken broth, mirin, shōyu, salt, and sugar. Bring to a boil, then simmer for about 3 minutes. Strain immediately. Save broth separately from other ingredients, and cool to room temperature.

Place 3 cups of the cooled broth with rice in rice cooker. When rice is done (about one hour), cook peas in microwave just until bright green, approximately 2 minutes. Mix cooked vegetables, peas, and chicken with the rice. Serve hot or at room temperature.

Serves 6

Gohan

The Japanese take comfort in a bowl of steaming gohan (rice). Gohan is so central to the culture that it is also the word for "meal."

Issei women who were in charge of feeding vast crews of farm workers in the fertile land of the Central Valley of California always cooked huge pots of gohan with the hearty lunches. When it was ready they would call out to the field, "GOHAN!" The field hands, whether Japanese, Mexican or Filipino would then drop their tools and rush to the common lunch hall for a bountiful spread.

My dad used to say that anyone who shares our gohan pot with us is a friend forever. He had many friends.

My parents resettled in Omaha, Nebraska, after being released from an internment camp. I was born and raised in Omaha. About 25 of us Nikkei families lived there and gohan was central to our lives. We, as young children, were weaned on okayu (rice porridge).

Every year one of the members of the families would be designated to rent a huge semi-truck and drive to Arkansas, two states away, to stock up on hundred-pound sacks of rice, a year's supply of real "okome." This load was then distributed to the 25 families.

I remember that toward the end of the year we would find small black flecks floating up to the surface from the washed okome. They were mouse droppings. The rice was too precious to throw away. The women agreed that the mice were harmless and that the gohan was safe to eat after the droppings were scooped off and the rice "sterilized" in the boiling water. The gohan tasted just as good, so we kids were not squeamish about it.

The love for gohan is being perpetuated in our community as we learn that nori and Spam musubi are the best sellers to the younger generation at Japantown lunch counters.

—KAREN FUJII, AS TOLD TO KIKU FUNABIKI

Most Japanese know what a treat matsutake is for autumn. The woody fragrance is quite distinct. Mom grew up in the Pacific Northwest where these delicacies grew wild in the mountains. This recipe can probably be applied to rice cookers, but Mom didn't believe in them until only recently.

– MIDORI YENARI

Matsutake Gohan (Pine Mushroom Rice)

     3 cups Japanese style rice
  3½ cups water
     1 piece of konbu or ½ teaspoon instant dashi
     3 Tablespoons shōyu
        Tablespoon sake
   ½ teaspoon salt
        6-ounce matsutake

Wash rice (9 times or until wash water is clear). Drain for and set aside for 1 hour. Wash and chop matsutake into small pieces. Bring rice, water, konbu, shōyu, and sake to a boil. Add salt and matsutake reduce heat and steam for 30 minutes. Turn off heat. Let stand for 10 minutes before serving.

One of my fondest memories is my dad hovering around the kitchen table while my mom was still cooking. He would nibble on bits of food, smacking his lips and making appreciative sounds and comments way before it was time to eat. He was having appetizers, long before we knew what appetizers were. What we did know was that he loved my mom's cooking so much he just couldn't wait to eat!

I remember one of the first times I attempted to make inarizushi, my mother remarked "Oh my! Shōyu must have been on sale!," referring to the sushi's dark brown color. From then on, I used her recipe.

– BEATRICE ITO

Mom's Inarizushi (Cone or Pouch Sushi)

6 aburage packages
   Hot water

Age sauce:

2 cups dashi
½ cup sugar
1 Tablespoon salt
   Shōyu, for color

Cut age into halves, forming pockets. Boil in water and drain age pieces to remove excess oil. Repeat. Simmer age in sauce for about 30 minutes or until broth is almost gone. Drain. Cool. Fill age pockets with sushi rice. Makes 12 inarizushi.

Camp Cravings

After a year of dull "camp fare"—canned beans, Spam, rutabagas, "slop suey," heavy with fats and starches—Mother longed for unagi. She craved charcoal-grilled eel just as teenagers today yearned for hamburgers and Coke. She even dreamed of unagi which would never grace a messhall table. She remembered what a delicacy it was in Japan.

My father worked in the camp messhall and was moved by Mama's obsession. One night, he took my brother mysteriously into the night, not stating where they were going. They were out late and returned after the family had gone to bed.

The family didn't learn until the next day of the night's adventure. Papa and brother took great risks in clandestinely sneaking past the guard by crawling under the barbed wire fence. They were now in forbidden area armed with a wooden club and a sack. Moving with stealth and keeping one eye on the watch-tower they lured a rattlesnake from its lair and clubbed it to death. With their victorious bounty they quickly sneaked back into the compound and found their way into the messhall, skinned the snake, marinated the meat then broiled it. There was no way to suppress the strong odor.

Mama was served like a queen on a table fashioned out of orange crates in our barrack. She was very touched by this loving expression by her usually stern, non-demonstrative issei husband.

Mama approached the substitute gingerly and took a nibble. She said it was a bit gamey, but not bad.

–Kiku Funabiki

Grandma's Five-O Rice

My sons have had the benefit of having their grandma and grandpa "downstairs" from the day they were born. There were many meals and many memories, but my youngest son, Barry, remembers grandma's fried rice. When he was little, he understood her to be saying "five-o" when she asked if he wanted fried rice. He figured it must have been some kind of Hawai'ian recipe since grandma lived in Hawai'i for a while.

–Judy Yoko Hamaguchi

Five-O Rice

Any amount of cooked rice; leftovers work well
Bacon, Spam, or hot dogs, diced
Half block of kamaboko, diced
1 yellow onion, diced
Salt to taste
Shōyu to taste
2 or 3 eggs, beaten
Green onions, sliced

Fry the diced bacon in a large skillet. Add yellow onions and brown with bacon. Add kamaboko and continue cooking. Add your cooked rice and stir up together. Add salt and shōyu to taste. Pour the beaten eggs over the rice and mix together. Add the green onions when the fried rice is almost done. Fried rice should not be tacky feeling, but just moist. Serve with tsukemono.

This recipe is based on my memory of my mother's sabazushi on New Year's Day—
the look and taste of it, and how I used to enjoy it. Whenever I make it now, I think of
my issei parents from Wakayama-ken—my mother who used to make the sushi and
my father who was once a fisherman in San Pedro.

– Hiroshi Kashiwagi

Sabazushi (Allow several days to prepare)

- 1 medium to large (1½ pounds) mackerel
  Salt
- 2½ cups of rice (use small measuring cup from the rice cooker)

Sweet vinegar marinade:
- ¼ cup white vinegar
- ¼ cup rice vinegar
- ½ cup sugar
- ½ teaspoon salt

Use one saba, mackerel; the Norwegian frozen ones are best because of their
consistent quality. Allow a day or two to defrost.

When thawed remove head and tail, split, and gut the fish. Also, remove the
backbone; you will have two pieces of saba which you salt heavily; the salt should
be visible on the surface; refrigerate for two or three days.

Bathe the fish in cold water for 15 minutes or so; repeat this process once.
This is quite a tricky procedure; do not remove all the salt.

Make the sweet vinegar marinade. In a pot, combine marinade ingredients.
Stir and heat until the liquid is clear, the sugar and salt having dissolved; cool
before using. Pat fish pieces dry. Starting at the edge, carefully peel away the outer
translucent skin. Carefully remove all the bones; be sure to get all the little bones
in the center. Pour half the vinegar marinade over the fish to cover; leave a little
marinade for the sushi rice. Refrigerate the saba for at least two days.

Cook the rice a bit dryer than usual. While the rice is hot, sprinkle some vinegar marinade (not too much), mix and cool vigorously while fanning. Spread half the rice on a sheet of waxed paper; pat dry one fish, place it over the rice, wrap into a roll with the wax paper, and put it in the sushi box or press. Repeat this process with the other piece of fish. Now, you will have two rolls of sushi in the box that you press overnight with a weight. Before slicing the sushi, trim the edges to make it look more attractive.

Pea Gohan

 4 cups rice
 5 cups water
 1 pound, unshelled fresh English peas (1 cup)
2½ teaspoons salt

Wash the rice. Add peas, salt, and appropriate amount of water. Cook. Let settle for 12 to 15 minutes before serving.

Serves 4 to 6

TŌFU SURPRISE

San Jose Tōfu

San Jose Tōfu comes as an eye-opener to those who think tōfu is just tōfu. In an age of processed and mass-produced foods, the tōfu made by Takeshi Nozaki is still made by hand, using slow, traditional methods and equipment. One taste of his freshly made squares—there are no preservatives, so it has to be eaten soon—reveals just how good tōfu can be.

Mr. Nozaki makes blocks of momen, or "cotton," tōfu. Firmer than kinugoshi ("silk") but softer than the Chinese variety, momen tōfu is the standard Japanese type for day-to-day use. Unlike commercially produced tōfu, Mr. Nozaki uses nigari, or brine solution, to solidify the soy milk that will become tōfu. Most of the tōfu is sold directly from the shop, but some goes to local restaurants and specialty grocery stores. To those who request it, the shop also sells okara, the soybean pulp or lees that is a by-product of the tōfu-making process and high in dietary fiber and protein. The main okara customers, however, are pig farmers who use it for feed.

Since its founding in 1947, San Jose Tōfu has been at the same location on Jackson Street in San Jose, California's Japantown. The making of the tōfu has remained the same, but the clientele has changed over the years. From the 1950s to the mid-70s, virtually all the customers were from the Japanese community. With the growing appreciation of tōfu as a health food and the growth of the nearby San Jose downtown and Civic Center, the customers who flock to San Jose Tōfu represent a wide variety of races and ethnic backgrounds. Everyone can appreciate the delicious, fresh and nutritious qualities of the Nozakis' tōfu.

–PAT ABE-CALEF

Tōfu Casserole

1 block regular tōfu, sliced lengthwise about ¾ inch wide
1 pound ground pork
2 Tablespoons sake
¼ cup shōyu
2 Tablespoons brown sugar
1½ inch piece of ginger, peeled and chopped
1 clove garlic, minced
¼ cup shiitake, soaked and diced
¼ cup onion, diced
¼ cup bamboo shoots, diced
¼ cup green onion, sliced
7 to 8 water chestnuts, diced
2 beaten eggs

Preheat oven 350 degrees. Slice tōfu. Lay pieces on bottom of lightly greased casserole. Sauté pork, ginger, and garlic. Add shiitake, bamboo shoots, onions, water chestnuts, sake, shōyu, and sugar. Pour mixture over tōfu in casserole dish. Spread chopped green onions over mixture. Pour beaten eggs over entire mixture. Bake for 35 to 45 minutes.

Crab Bean Cake Quiche

1	block tōfu
1	6-ounce can crab
1	medium carrot, cut in long thin strips
3 to 4	shiitake, softened in warm water
2	pieces fresh or canned bamboo shoots
3 to 4	stalks green onion
	Frozen green peas, as desired
2 to 3	inch piece of ginger, chopped or grated
10	eggs
2	Tablespoons oil
1	Tablespoon shōyu
1	Tablespoon sugar
1	Tablespoon sake
½	teaspoon salt, divided in half

Preheat oven to 350 degrees. Mash tōfu and put in boiling water. When tōfu rises, take out and drain on towel. Slice the vegetables in thin long strips. Defrost frozen peas by rinsing in hot water. Stir fry vegetables, except the peas, in oil. Add shōyu, sugar, sake, and ¼ teaspoon salt. Add tōfu, peas and crab. Beat 10 eggs and add ¼ teaspoon salt. Add tōfu, crab, and vegetables to egg mixture. Pour into greased square baking dish. Bake until toothpick comes out clean, about 30 minutes. Take out of oven and loosen around the edges with a knife. Cool for about 5 minutes. Slice to about 32 pieces. Remove from pan before it completely cools and arrange on a platter.

Tōfu Patties

1 Tablespoon oil (for pan)

1 block regular tōfu

1 cup mung bean sprouts

1 bunch green onions, sliced

2 Tablespoons mochi flour (or one egg)

¾ cup okara

⅓ cup oatmeal

¼ cup oat bran

Dash of cayenne

Dash of ground ginger

1 teaspoon salt

1 Tablespoon shōyu

¼ teaspoon sugar

1 Tablespoon, roasted, ground goma

Squeeze excess water out of the tōfu using a cheesecloth or thin dish towel. Break up tōfu. Parboil (or microwave) bean sprouts until tender. Squeeze excess water from bean sprouts when cool, and chop roughly. In a large bowl, combine all ingredients together and mix well. Heat oil in skillet. Form golf-ball sized balls of the mixture, flatten in pan, and fry until golden brown.

Shira-ae

½ block tōfu

1 bunch spinach

2 Tablespoons miso

½ teaspoon ajinomoto (optional)

1 teaspoon toasted sesame seeds

1 Tablespoon sugar

Slice tōfu in thirds. Place tōfu in clean cloth and squeeze to remove excess water. Cut off root ends of the spinach. Wash spinach well. In boiling water, put whole spinach in and take out immediately so as not to overcook. Dip spinach in cool water. Squeeze out excess water and chop into bite size sections. In suribachi, grind toasted seeds and miso. Add sugar and ajinomoto to taste. Add tōfu and mix well. Lastly, add chopped spinach.

Variation: Substitute spinach and seeds for 1 Tablespoon peanut butter, 2 Tablespoons sugar, and juice of half a lemon. You can add cooked napa, green beans, or broccoli. Cucumbers can be used if seeded, sliced thin, salted, then washed again. Sliced abalone makes an excellent garnish.

Tuna Okara Balls

1 6-ounce can tuna, drained

1 cup okara, packed

3 eggs

¼ cup milk

6 water chestnuts, chopped

½ cup chopped onion

Oil for frying

1 teaspoon salt

Black pepper to taste

Combine all ingredients. Shape teaspoonful of mixture into balls or patties. Cook in deep fat until golden brown. Drain on paper towel. Serve hot or at room temperature.

Note: If you want larger patties you can refrigerate before frying and also coat patties with panko for easier handling while cooking.

Tōfu Salad

1 10-ounce block tōfu, cubed

1 sweet onion, sliced

1 7.5-ounce can salmon

1 tomato, sliced

Sauce:

½ cup vegetable oil

1 clove garlic, minced

½ cup shōyu

3 stalks green onion, minced

Gently mix together tōfu, onions, salmon, and tomato in a serving dish. Heat oil with garlic; add shōyu and green onions. Stir, then cool slightly. Pour over tōfu salad just before serving.

Tōfu Pie

1 graham cracker pie crust
1 3-ounce package Jello, lime or any fruit flavor
1 cup hot water
½ block soft tōfu, crumbled
1 8-ounce tub Cool Whip
2 Tablespoons lemon juice

Combine Jello with hot water in a medium bowl, stirring until dissolved. Place in blender; add tōfu and blend together. Add lemon juice. Fold in ½ of the Cool Whip until mixed and smooth. Pour into prepared pie crust and refrigerate until firm. The pie can be made the night before and refrigerated overnight. When firm, spread remainder of the Cool Whip on top of pie. Refrigerate until ready to serve. Store any leftover pie in refrigerator.

Chocolate Dream Dessert

12 ounces semi-sweet chocolate chips
2 Tablespoons water
2 packages extra firm tōfu
1 teaspoon vanilla
1 large banana
1 graham cracker pie crust
 Almond slices, optional

Melt chocolate in microwave oven with water. Thoroughly blend tōfu in a blender or food processor. Add melted chocolate and vanilla to the tōfu and blend at a high speed for 2 minutes.

Slice banana and layer with chocolate mixture in either pudding cups or graham cracker pie crust. Refrigerate 1 to 2 hours. Garnish with remaining banana slices and almond slices, if desired.

VINEGARED FAVORITES

Instant Takuan Tsukemono (Pickled Radish)

8 quarts daikon (thick and short is the best!) cut into bite-sized pieces, about 2 x ½ inches

Sauce:

4 ½ cups sugar

1 cup white vinegar

½ cup salt

½ teaspoon yellow food coloring

Place cut daikon in large pan or bowl. Mix sauce ingredients. Pour vinegar mixture over daikon. Allow to stand overnight; liquid should cover daikon. Pack in jars with a sprinkle of crushed red chili pepper. Refrigerate. Can be eaten in a few days.

Makes 4 ½ quarts.

Aloha Zuke

3 or 4 Japanese cucumbers

1 Tablespoon salt

1 teaspoon dry mustard

3 to 4 cloves garlic, diced

1 to 2 red chili peppers, chopped

2 ½ Tablespoons Japanese vinegar

1 ½ teaspoons ajinomoto, optional

Slice cucumber to bite size. Mix with rest of the ingredients. Refrigerate. Green cabbage or Chinese cabbage can also be used.

Nasubi Kōko (Pickled Eggplant)

2 to 3 Japanese eggplant
   2 Tablespoons sugar
   2 Tablespoons sake or whisky
   1 teaspoon dry mustard

Cut eggplant into slices. Sprinkle with salt. Let stand. Mix mustard with enough water to form a paste. Add the other ingredients to mustard mixture. Squeeze out the water from eggplant slices. Mix eggplant with mustard mixture. Let stand for 2 hours before serving.

Pickled Garlic

¾ cup distilled white vinegar
 2 Tablespoons sugar
¼ teaspoon hot chili flakes
¼ teaspoon black peppercorns
¼ teaspoon cumin seed
1 cup large garlic cloves, peeled

In a 1 or 1½ quart pan, combine vinegar, sugar, chili flakes, peppercorns, and cumin seed. Bring to a boil over high heat.

Add garlic cloves and return to a boil; simmer, uncovered, for two minutes. Pour the mixture into a jar. Cover, cool, and chill at least 24 hours or up to one month.

The Pacific Northwest area has been well known for its abundant growth of matsutake, pine mushrooms, since the issei pioneers worked in the forests and sawmills at the turn of the century and early 1900s era. The matsutake can no longer be harvested as plentifully as in the past due to the clearing and logging out of the many forests. However, we still take one or two trips a year in the fall to "our favorite hunting grounds" in search of the diminishing growth of the prized matsutake.

Favorite uses of the matsutake are in soups, batter fried, or in sukiyaki. Its "piney" aroma adds a most pleasing taste to the palate.

–KIKU MORITA, TACOMA BUDDHIST WOMEN'S ASSOCIATION

Matsutake Sanbaizuke

1 quart matsutake, sliced

Sauce A:
¾ cup sake (Japanese rice wine)
¼ cup vinegar
½ cup shōyu
¼ cup mirin
2 Tablespoons sugar

Sauce B: (sweeter)
½ cup sake
¼ cup vinegar
½ cup shōyu
½ cup sugar

Boil the above sauce ingredients in a pot. Add 1 quart sliced matsutake and bring to a boil. Remove from heat and store in a clean jar, covered with plastic wrap and then a lid. It will store up to 1 year in the refrigerator.

Aburage Namasu (Fried Tōfu Salad)

    1 can or package ajitsuke aburage, seasoned and ready to use for inari sushi
    ½ cup water
2 to 3 bundles sōmen, cooked
    1 tray prepared seaweed salad
    1 small tray imitation crab
    3 Tablespoons sugar
    2 Tablespoons rice vinegar
    1 Tablespoon sesame oil

In a pot, cook aburage with water for 5 minutes. Drain and cut into small pieces. Combine with remaining ingredients. Chill and serve.

Cucumber Sunomono (Cucumber Salad)

    2 Japanese or 1 seedless cucumber
    ¼ pound shrimp, uncooked
    2 strips wakame
    3 Tablespoons vinegar
    1 Tablespoon sugar
    1 teaspoon shōyu

Thinly slice cucumber. Sprinkle salt over cucumber, set aside for about 5 minutes. Gently knead cucumber and squeeze out water. Shell and devein shrimp. Quickly boil shrimp in water until pink. Drain and slice shrimp in halves. Soak wakame in water until soft. Cut into bite size pieces. Combine vinegar, sugar and shōyu, stirring well to dissolve the sugar. Toss together cucumber, shrimp, and wakame. Pour the dressing over all and mix thoroughly.

Daikon and Carrot Sunomono

   1 medium daikon

   ½ medium carrot

   1 piece lemon rind, 1 inch square

Dressing:

   ½ cup white vinegar

   ½ cup sugar

   1 teaspoon salt

Wash and pare daikon. Cut crosswise into ½ inch lengths. Cut each piece lengthwise into very thin slices. Stack the slices and cut into julienne strips. Wash, peel, and julienne the carrot. Wash and cut lemon rind into small, thin strips. Combine dressing ingredients in a small saucepan. Heat until sugar dissolves. In a bowl, add dressing to taste to salad mixture. Mix well. Refrigerate. Stir occasionally. Tastes best if you make it 1 to 2 days in advance.

Note: For convenience, you can use the vinegar mixture for sushi rice.

Kurome Namasu (Seaweed Salad)

   1 large carrot

   1 medium daikon

   3 pieces aburage

   1 1.5-ounce package kurome

Sauce:

   ½ cup white vinegar

   ¾ cup sugar

   1 Tablespoon salt

   3 Tablespoons roasted sesame seeds

Cut daikon and carrot into matchstick strips. Pour boiling water on aburage in a bowl and soak for about 5 minutes to take out the oil. Squeeze water out and cut into strips. Wash and clean kurome. Soak for 10–15 minutes and drain. Mix all ingredients well and serve cold.

This dish was served so graciously at Mrs. Yamada's home in Palolo Valley, Hawai'i. She said her children didn't like the tart taste of the usual namasu sauce so she uses seasoned vinegar instead. The dried fungus ears turned out crunchy but I first thought it was ogo (seaweed)!

–Valerie Tanaka

Cucumber and Carrot Namasu

½ cup seasoned vinegar
¾ cup sugar
1 Tablespoon salt
1 Tablespoon sesame seeds, toasted
1 teaspoon ajinomoto, optional
1 can boiled baby clams, drained
1 to 2 cucumbers, peeled and sliced thinly
1 carrot, peeled and sliced thin
¼ cup dried wakame, soaked
¼ cup sliced dried fungus ears, soaked and sliced

Combine vinegar, sugar, salt, sesame seeds, ajinomoto, and clams in a jar and shake. Toss with the last 4 ingredients.

Hasu Namasu (Lotus Root Salad)

1 medium hasu, peeled, sliced and parboiled
1 can hokkigai (seasoned baby clams)
1 white onion, sliced thinly

Sauce:
1 cup rice vinegar
1 cup white sugar
1 heaping Tablespoon salt
1 teaspoon ajinomoto, optional
Ginger, slivered
Shōyu to color

Combine sauce ingredients. Add sliced hasu, hokkigai, and onions. Chill and serve.

MOCHI DELIGHTS

Girls' Day Mochi

The first time I made apricot mochi was for my daughter Kellie Kaori Iwasaki's first Girls' Day in 1995. Since then, I make it often for potlucks and family gatherings and, of course, for celebrating Girls' Day.

– Patsy Nakayama Iwasaki

Apricot Mochi

>   1 box mochiko
>   2 3-ounce boxes apricot Jello
> 1½ cups sugar
>   1 11.5-ounce can Kern's apricot nectar
> 1½ cups water

Preheat oven to 350 degrees. Mix ingredients together well. Dissolving all lumps. Pour into greased 9 x 13 inch pan. Cover with foil. Bake for 55 minutes. Remove from oven. Remove foil after 15 minutes. Cut into bite-size pieces after it cools. Sprinkle with cornstarch or kinako.

Variation:
Peach Jello and peach nectar can be used instead of apricot.

Camellia Mochi

2½ rice cooker cups mochigome
1 to 2 drops red food coloring
5 Tablespoons sugar
½ teaspoon salt
1 boiled egg yolk, mashed through sieve
1 12-ounce can prepared tsubushi or koshi an
20 camellia leaves, washed

Wash rice and add 2½ rice cooker cups water and the food coloring. Soak at least two hours. Cook in rice cooker. Transfer rice to bowl. Add sugar and salt and mash slightly with suribachi (mortar) stick. Flatten rice in hand moistened with water and wrap around a rounded teaspoonful of an. Make indentation on top and fill with drop of egg yolk. Place on camellia leaf. Makes 20 to 24.

Baked Chichi Dango

2 10-ounce packages mochiko
3 cups granulated sugar
1 12-ounce can coconut milk or 1½ cup condensed milk
2 cups water
1 Tablespoon miso
 Food coloring (red or orange)

Combine mochiko and sugar. Add mixture of coconut milk, miso, and water. Blend well with beater or whip. Add food coloring. Pour into well-oiled 9 x 13 pan. Cover securely with foil. Bake in 350 degree oven for 1 hour.

Take out of oven but leave foil on for 15 minutes only. Cool overnight uncovered or until cold, about 4 hours. Use plastic knife to cut and use cornstarch to coat.

Note: If using 13 ounce can of coconut milk, add water to leftover coconut milk to make 2 cups water in recipe.

Mochi Cake

  1 16-ounce box mochiko
  1 teaspoon baking soda
  2 cups brown sugar
  1 12-ounce can coconut milk
1½ cups water
  1 12-ounce can tsubushi an
    Vegetable oil

Preheat oven to 350 degrees. Mix mochiko, baking soda, and brown sugar. Add coconut milk, and water, and mix well. Stir in an. Grease a 9 x 13 pan with vegetable oil and sprinkle sesame seeds on bottom of pan. Pour in batter and sprinkle sesame seeds on top. Bake for 1 hour or longer if necessary, until inserted knife comes out clean. Cool before cutting.

Mochiko Chews

  5 cups mochiko
1½ cups brown sugar
  2 12-ounce cans coconut milk, thawed if frozen
  1 12-ounce can water
  1 teaspoon baking soda

Preheat oven to 350 degrees. Mix all ingredients and pour into a 9 x 13 baking pan. Bake for about an hour. Insert knife, which should come out clean. Cut when cool.

Microwave Habutae Mochi

1½ cups mochiko (mochi flour)

1½ cups water

½ cup sugar

   Katakuriko

1 12-ounce can tsubushi an

Mix mochiko, water, and sugar in bowl. Lightly coat small microwave tube cake pan with cooking spray. Microwave 3 minutes on low (50% power), 3 minutes on medium (70% power), then 3 minutes on high.

While hot, turn mochi onto teflon-coated baking pan sprinkled with katakuriko (potato starch). Sprinkle top of mochi with katakuriko. Cut mochi into 14 pieces. Dust hands with starch and flatten each piece. Place 1 Tablespoon tsubushi an (black bean paste) in center; bring edges together and pinch to seal. Shape as desired.

Variations:

Add fresh strawberry, peanut butter, or sweet chestnut covered with tsubushi an.

For chocolate mochi, stir in ½ cup of melted chocolate chips in batter before microwaving.

Add a few drops of food coloring, if desired, in batter before microwaving for color variation.

Or cut into pieces while hot and coat with kinako (soybean flour).

Use peanut butter (smooth or chunky), chocolate kisses, etc., according to individual taste.

Peanut Butter Microwave Mochi

1 cup sugar

1½ cups mochiko

1½ cups water

Yellow food coloring

1 18-ounce jar peanut butter

½ cup kinako, with sugar to taste

Mix the sugar, mochiko, and water together. Add a few drops of yellow food coloring. Spray a microwavable bundt pan with cooking spray. Pour mixture in bundt pan. Cover with plastic wrap. Microwave on high for five minutes. Then microwave on medium for two minutes; cooking times may differ according to your microwave. Take mochi mixture out of bundt pan by inverting pan onto a plate. Cut mochi into 16 pieces. Flatten each piece with your hand and put a spoonful of peanut butter in the middle. Wrap the mochi around the peanut butter. Roll the peanut butter mochi in a mixture of kinako mixed with a little sugar.

Baked Manjū

    6½ cups flour
    2 teaspoons baking soda
    2 Tablespoons sugar
    1 cup butter
    3 eggs
    1 5-ounce can evaporated milk
    1½ teaspoon vanilla
    1 12-ounce can koshi an or tsubushi an*

Sift flour, baking soda, and sugar. Cut in butter until the texture is mealy. Add eggs, milk, and vanilla, and blend thoroughly. Shape dough into small rounds using approximately a Tablespoon of dough. Flatten into circles and place about 2 teaspoons an in middle of circle. Pinch edges of dough together. Place seam side down on ungreased cookie sheet. Bake for 20 to 25 minutes in a 350 degree oven.

* Koshi an is a fine red bean paste; tsubushi an is coarser in texture and beans are only partially mashed.

Manjū

    5 cups flour
    1 teaspoon salt
    2 Tablespoons sugar
    2 cups oil
    ¾ cup chilled water
    1 12-ounce can tsubushi an

Preheat oven to 400 degrees. Blend flour, salt, and sugar thoroughly. Add oil and water to dry ingredients and mix well. Divide dough into 4 parts. Divide each part to yield 7 to 8 pieces. Flatten each piece with your hand and spoon an onto the center. Pinch ends to close over an. Place on lightly greased jelly roll pan. Brush the top of the dough with beaten egg white. Dot with red food coloring on the center. Bake for 15 to 25 minutes or until lightly browned.

COMFORT SPECIALS

Shiro Miso Soup, Colorado Style

6 Tablespoons Shiro (white) miso paste

6 cups water

1 3.5-ounce package dashi

1 Tablespoon mirin

1 teaspoon sugar

2 Tablespoons chopped white onion

¼ cup finely sliced green onions

1 cup tōfu, diced into ½ inch cubes

Bring water to a boil in a 2 to 4 quart sauce pan. Reduce heat slightly. Add dashi and stir. Using a small (3 inches diameter) metal strainer, mash the shiro miso paste through the strainer into the hot water. (Hint: do a little at a time and mash with strainer and miso in the heated broth.) Add the mirin, sugar, white onion, and tōfu. Add optional ingredient(s)—experiment with them as far as combinations and quantities are concerned. Use mild flavor fish for best results. Continue to heat all ingredients on medium heat for about 10 minutes. Garnish with a sprinkling of sliced green onions just prior to serving. Serve hot in Japanese lacquer bowl for authenticity; however, any soup bowl will work. Sipping from the bowl is allowed. Not for the faint at heart or the traditionalists: serve with Tabasco on the side.

Variations:

¼ cup pieces of white such as sea bass

or

½ cup sliced daikon

or

¼ cup cut wakame pieces, soaked

or

¼ cup thinly sliced age

or

½ cup sliced napa cabbage

My mother, born and raised in Nakagusuku, Okinawa, came to Hawaiʻi as a teenager to work the sugar cane fields of Hawaiʻi for 50 cents a day. However, she was able to save enough money from her meager earnings to send a small amount of money every year to relatives back home to buy land. I did not know this until she died. Going through her letters with a friend who could read Japanese, I discovered that my mother had, at one time, 18 parcels of land, one parcel for each year she worked in the cane fields. As it turned out, the parcels were not small; they were, in fact, large parcels of land. If my mother had claimed all her land in Okinawa, she would have been shocked to know that she had been a tycoon at one time! For all of her life, however, she lived as though she was still earning 50 cents a day. The following recipes are, therefore, the simplest of recipes, a fitting symbol of the simple life she lived.

– JULIA ESTRELLA

Egg in Rice

As soon as rice is cooked, place rice in chawan. Dig a hole in the hot rice and crack an egg into the opening. Drip shōyu over the egg according to taste and mix well with rice. Hot rice will cook some of the egg white but not all. For variation, add kimchee or pickled radish. Uncooked egg white is probably not good for the stomach but somehow generations of Japanese Americans using this recipe have survived to a ripe old age. My mother died at age 96.

Tuna Spaghetti

Boil one package of sōmen noodles; drain. Open can of tuna (oil pack tastes better) and sauté with minced onions. Add cooked and drained sōmen noodles into mixture and stir together. Tastes wonderful plain or add one can tomato sauce to mimic spaghetti. It was a custom of my mother to serve this dish every Sunday night for many, many years. We never got tired of it!

In a theoretical framework I think that shōyu hot dogs embody the perfect integration of both the Japanese (hence the shōyu) and American (hot dogs!!!) cultures. For my younger brother and me, it was the perfect dish to eat with gohan (although my brother tends to favor onigiri balls) and broccoli—can't forget the Miracle Whip! For me, it was the quintessential dish to make for those of us "I-love-cup-of-noodles-cause-it's-easy-to-make" types!!! It is amazing how such a simple dish has created so many memorable moments. When I think of shōyu hot dogs, I think of May's Coffee Shop breakfasts with the Kono relatives in San Francisco, and my brother's trips to and from Boston for school. My brother and I still anticipate those shōyu hot dog breakfasts at May's on those once a year trips that we make to San Francisco to visit my grandma and relatives. Our breakfasts have also become a time for family to get together and partake in the traditional passing of the orange slices to grandma! To us Chicagoans, it's such a treat to be able to eat our fave dish in a restaurant, something that hot dog stands back home definitely don't serve you!!! It has also become one of my brother's favorite dishes, so much so that my mother finds herself mass producing shōyu hot dogs and onigiri obentō's for my brother's arduous trips back to school. Hmmm . . . this could turn into a family business!

– Erika Kono

Shōyu Hot Dogs

    1 green pepper
½ onion
    1 package hot dogs (for good flavor, use Chicago Kosher hot dogs!!)
       Brown sugar to taste
       Shōyu to taste

Chop onions and green peppers and sauté until limp. Set aside. Fry sliced hot dogs until slightly brown. Add shōyu and brown sugar to hot dog mixture and cook on medium high heat. Add additional brown sugar to taste, or until sauce consistency is semi thick. Add onions and green peppers. Simmer on low heat.

Picnic Egg

I found that eggs were the least expensive way of providing protein for our family of seven. Eggs were often on sale for 39 cents a dozen! Of course, we all loved what we called "egg on rice," which was a raw egg and shōyu mixed with hot rice. (Didn't know about salmonella, and still ignore that knowledge now.) Lloyd concocted what we started calling "rolled up egg," which was an egg, beaten, poured out in a thin layer in a hot skillet, and rolled up. He remembered his brother Bill using Girard's salad dressing on his eggs, so that's what we used on rolled up egg. This reminded me of one of the few things I remember as Mama's specialties, besides osushi and ozōni, what our family called "picnic rolled up egg." It became our favorite item to take on picnics. I remember seeing her doing this:

Beat well about 8 eggs in a bowl, seasoning to taste with salt and shōyu. Cut a small piece from an old sheet, fold it into a small dish, soak lightly in vegetable oil. Heat to hot a thin layer of vegetable oil in a heavy medium sized skillet (iron is best). Lower heat slightly and pour a thin layer of the beaten egg to cover the skillet bottom. This cooks very quickly and in order that it will stick while rolling, immediately start tightly rolling with ohashi (chopstick) from bottom to top of pan away from yourself.

Immediately add another thin layer of beaten egg. When cooked through but still sticky, tightly roll up. As the skillet's oil is used up (might be every few layers of egg), use ohashi to pick up the oil-ladened piece of cloth and wipe a thin layer on bottom of pan. Continue until the roll is about the size of a roll of makizushi. Set aside to cool. Slice all the rolls a little thinner than makizushi and pack into your obentō bako with other goodies to eat on your picnic, or obentō when traveling.

On a recent car trip to L.A., having only a small amount of sliced teriyaki type meats, we took this for our obentō with rice balls, ajitsukenori, oshōga, okōko, and other tsukemono. Our grandson there enjoyed the leftovers!

–Marion Wake

My mother, a pediatrician, would often bring home some "leftover catch" or "omiyage" from a friend or a patient of hers. Ideally, we tried to eat the seafood right away, because we knew how fresh it was. This is one of the dishes we enjoyed "Japanese style," using local seafood.

—Midori Yenari

Katsu Oikawa Yenari Broiled Soft Shell Crabs

1 dozen soft shell crabs (these are the blue crabs found in the Gulf of Mexico or the Chesapeake Bay)

Marinade:
¼ cup shōyu
1 Tablespoon sake
½ Tablespoon sugar
About 1 teaspoon fresh lemon juice

Mix marinade ingredients and pour over crabs. Marinate for an hour or overnight. Turn broiler to 500 degrees. Lightly salt and pepper the crabs and place on a broiling rack in a pan (to catch drippings). Broil in the oven for 1 to 2 minutes, then turn over and broil again. Baste with remaining sauce.

Konnyaku with Clams

1 10-ounce package konnyaku
1 6-ounce can ajitsuke kogai, undrained
3 Tablespoons lemon juice
2 teaspoons shōyu

Cut konnyaku in half lengthwise. Slice into ½ inch thick pieces. Add remaining ingredients and mix well. Chill before serving.

Mama's Wine

Papa sold insurance to farmers and was often paid in lugs of vegetables and fruit. One day, crates of grapes were unloaded from his 1920-something clunker. Too abundant for table consumption, Mama asked our Italian fish peddler how wine could be made from the grapes—they communicated in immigrant English. The peddler was delighted to show her. He wasted no time and began the process by filling our large tsukemono crock with the grapes, unwashed. To Mama's horror he stepped into the crock with his boots, fish scales still clinging to them. He then proceeded to crush the fruit until the juices rose above the mash, to which he added sugar, then stirred gently. After several weeks there bubbled up a muddy concoction which Mama filtered and decanted. My brothers and I were given a sip of this when we caught colds. I loved the sweet, full taste and the warm glow it gave my congested chest. I remember the coughs we faked just to get a sip of this murky treat.

–Kiku Funabiki

POT LUCK

The Art of Communal Feasting

Camp Moonshiners

In June 1986, a pilgrimage for ex-internees of Heart Mountain internment center was held at the old site. It drew about a hundred of us for a reunion and for a dedication of a memorial for veterans of World War II who gave their lives to the country.

After the formal ceremonies, we gathered in Cody, a small town outside the camp site. Swapping stories after lunch turned out to be the high point of the trip. One Nisei man enjoyed a captive audience as he told of his exploits of running an elaborate still he had constructed under his unit. He had laboriously and surreptitiously dug a basement under the barrack, carefully bracing the ceiling with railroad ties. He had even designed an escape route in the event of a raid!

He then hand-built a still with copper tubing. All the materials were collected from "midnight inventories," covert operations during the night raiding warehouses. Raw materials were the easiest to procure from willing cohorts in the mess halls. Raisins and prunes never found their way to the table since they always seemed to be diverted to the moonshiners. Our raconteur openly told us that there was heavy competition throughout the camp. They must have kept their operations literally airtight since I never detected suspicious smells in my walks past the barracks. I was amused at the freedom and candor with which he related the stories since he was now "off the hook" after the forty or more years which had elapsed.

Inventiveness and resourcefulness were never in short demand to internees who had suddenly found themselves with leisure time.

–Kiku Funabiki

SOUPS AND SALADS

On cold winter evenings, Papa frequently asked Mama to cook his favorite Satsuma Jiru or Butadōfu. Both my parents were from Kagoshima-ken and they especially favored the good, hearty dishes for which Satsuma is famous. My husband Peter was fond of Satsuma Jiru and Butadōfu,* though his parents were not from Kagoshima. Our grown nisei children and my Caucasian friends also favor these tasty dishes.

– YOSHINO HASEGAWA

* Appears in the pot luck meat section of this book

Satsuma Jiru (Pork and Vegetables in Miso Soup)

½ pound pork, sliced into thin, bite size pieces
6 cups dashi
½ cup shiro miso
1 cup daikon, diced
2 cups satoimo, sliced

In saucepan, heat dashi. Add pork, miso (diluted and mixed with the dashi), daikon, and satoimo. Simmer 15 to 20 minutes until the pork is cooked and satoimo is soft.

Mock Bird's-Nest Soup

4 to 5 pieces of shiitake
1 package of long rice (sai fun) noodles
½ pound ground pork
2 large cans of chicken broth
1 small can water chestnuts, sliced or whole
1 egg, beaten
2 to 3 stalks of green onions, sliced

Soak shiitake mushrooms in warm water. Slice when mushroom is soft. Prepare long rice as directed on package. Stir-fry ground pork and drain on paper towel. Boil broth in pot and add a pinch of salt. Add water chestnuts, pork, and sliced mushrooms. Simmer. Before serving, add long rice and drizzle in 1 beaten egg. Garnish with green onions.

Many of our mothers and grandmothers used no written recipes in their cooking—just a pinch here and a dash there. Yet, those are the foods which we recall the most when we think of the best foods we grew up on. As we enjoy these recipes, we are so mindful of the important part that interdependence continues to play in our lives as it nourishes us fully from one generation to another.

–Palo Alto Buddhist Women's Association

Buta to Horensō no Misoshiru (Pork and Spinach Miso Soup)

⅔ cup miso

4 cups water

1 pound spinach, washed thoroughly

½ pound pork shoulder

1 stalk green onion, minced

Ginger, grated to taste

Dissolve miso paste in water. Cut spinach into one inch lengths and add to miso and water mixture. Cube meat into 2 inch pieces; then add to the soup. Cook soup until meat done. Remove from the burner and add green onions and ginger. Serve immediately.

Artichoke Salad

1 package Chicken or Almond Rice-A-Roni
1 8-ounce jar marinated artichokes
¼ cup bell pepper, chopped
3 stalks green onion, thinly sliced
½ can sliced black olives, drained
1 3.8-ounce can sliced water chestnuts, drained
⅓ cup mayonnaise
Chopped or sliced almonds

Prepare Rice-A-Roni according to package instructions. Let cool. Add other ingredients and chill.

Aunt Betty's Cabbage Salad

1 head cabbage, shredded
1 kamaboko, shredded
2 packages rāmen noodles, crushed
3 Tablespoons sesame seed, toasted
¼ cup green onions, sliced
⅓ cup toasted almonds, sliced

Salad Dressing:
¼ cup sesame oil
¼ cup salad oil
3 Tablespoons rice vinegar
3 Tablespoons sugar
½ teaspoon black pepper
1 package Good Season Italian Dressing

Mix all, except dressing ingredients and chill. Add dressing ingredients into a bottle and shake. Toss salad with dressing just before serving.

Cabbage Rāmen Salad I

2 cups cooked chicken breast

1 medium cabbage, finely shredded

4 Tablespoons green onions, chopped

4 Tablespoons sesame seeds, toasted

4 Tablespoons sliced almonds, toasted

1 package rāmen instant noodles, crushed

Dressing:

4 Tablespoons sugar

6 Tablespoons seasoned rice vinegar

1 teaspoon black pepper

¼ cup sesame oil

Bake or simmer chicken breasts in a saucepan with a little water and a piece of fresh ginger. Let cool and cube, slice, or shred. Set aside. Combine cabbage, onions, sesame seeds, almonds, and rāmen; add chicken. Toss and chill for ½ hour before serving. Pour dressing over salad and toss again before serving.

Serves 8 to 10

Cabbage Rāmen Salad II

  1 small head green cabbage, finely sliced

  ½ small head red cabbage, finely sliced

  2 pieces chicken breast, baked and shredded

  2 3-ounce Nissin Seasoned Rāmen packages, crumbled

  ¼ cup toasted sliced almonds or cashew nuts

  1 stalk green onion, thinly sliced

Dressing:

  ½ cup salad oil

  6 Tablespoons white vinegar

  4 Tablespoons sugar

  1 teaspoon salt

  ¼ teaspoon pepper

    Few drops sesame oil

  2 Tablespoons toasted sesame seeds

Combine all salad ingredients. Pour on dressing. Toss lightly and chill.

Serves 8 to 10

Chinese Chicken Salad I

- 1 head iceberg lettuce, shredded
- 2 stalks thin green onion, finely sliced
- 3 cups cooked chicken, shredded
- 1 bunch sai fun (rice) noodles, deep fried
- 1 package slivered almonds, toasted, optional

Dressing:

- 3 Tablespoons sugar
- 1 teaspoon salt
   - Dash ajinomoto, optional
- ½ teaspoon pepper
- ¼ cup salad oil
- 1 Tablespoon sesame oil
- 3 Tablespoon white vinegar
- ½ teaspoon dry mustard

Put dressing ingredients in a jar and shake. Toss salad ingredients together. Just before serving, pour dressing over salad, toss, and serve. For presentation, leave sai fun on top.

Serves 8 to 10

Chinese Chicken Salad II

2 chicken breasts, deboned and skinless

Marinade:

¼ cup shōyu

1 clove garlic, grated

1 slice of ginger (about the size of a quarter), minced

4 teaspoons sugar

Salad:

1 head lettuce, shredded

4 green onion stalks, slivered

½ cup celery, thinly sliced

1 bunch of cilantro (Chinese parsley), use leaf only and remove stems

½ cup sesame seed, toasted

½ cup dry roasted peanuts, chopped

Oil for frying

⅛ teaspoon celery salt

¼ teaspoon five spice powder

Dressing:

2 Tablespoons sugar

1 teaspoon salt

1 teaspoon ajinomoto, optional

¼ teaspoon pepper

¼ cup salad oil

1 Tablespoon sesame oil

3 Tablespoons rice vinegar

Marinate chicken breasts for about an hour. Mix vegetables, sesame seeds, and peanuts in large salad bowl. Deep fry chicken breasts in hot oil until golden brown. Remove and drain on paper towel. Cool chicken, shred into narrow strips. Add celery salt and five spice powder; mix and let stand about a minute. Add chicken and spice mixture to vegetables and lightly toss. Mix the salad dressing ingredients in a jar and shake until sugar is dissolved. Chill and pour over salad before serving.

Optional: Add 4 to 5 handfuls of fried Chinese rice sticks (sai fun or mei fun). To prepare, drop a small handful of rice sticks in very hot oil. As soon as they puff up, remove immediately with a wire strainer. They should be snow white, not browned. Drain on paper towel. Then add to above salad and lightly toss.

Serves 8 to 10

Everybody has a macaroni or potato salad recipe. Macaroni salad shows up at every pot luck and even New Year's parties. My grandma in Kealakekua, Hawai'i, had the most interesting and tasty versions. She added sliced canned abalone. She also tossed in seeded and sliced cucumbers. The cucumbers were sprinkled with salt, set aside, and then water was squeezed out. My Honolulu grandma added frozen carrots and peas defrosted under warm water. Mom likes tuna or canned crab in her salads. If you want the Hawai'i flavor, macaroni and potato are used together and no mustard or vinegar is added.

–GAYLE T. NISHIKAWA

Citrus Green Salad

- 1 head romaine lettuce
- 1 10.5-ounce can mandarin oranges, chilled and drained
- 4 to 5 thin slices sweet red onion
- ¼ pound fresh mushrooms, sliced
- 2 Tablespoons toasted sesame seeds
- 2 to 4 Tablespoons toasted sliced almonds

Dressing:
- ½ cup olive oil
- 2 Tablespoons tarragon vinegar
- 1 to 2 Tablespoons orange juice
- ½ teaspoon salt
- 2 Tablespoons sugar
- ½ teaspoon dry mustard
- ½ teaspoon celery salt
- 1 teaspoon grated onion
- ½ teaspoon grated orange rind

Combine dressing ingredients in a covered container. Shake well. Refrigerate. Tear romaine lettuce into a salad bowl. Add oranges, onion, mushrooms, and sesame seeds. Toss salad with dressing and sprinkle with almonds just before serving.

Serves 8 to 10

Broccoli and Raisin Salad

  3 bunches broccoli, cut into bite-size pieces (using just crowns is easier)

½ cup golden raisins

½ cup dried cranberries

¼ cup almonds, slivered

¼ cup red onion

⅛ cup green onion, slivered

  5 bacon slices, fried and crumbled

Dressing:

  2 cups mayonnaise

⅔ cup sugar

½ cup raspberry vinegar

Toss all the salad ingredients together. Mix dressing and shake well. Pour over salad. Let salad sit for a couple of minutes. Just before serving, toss again.

Harusame Salad

1 package harusame (Japanese sai fun)

2 eggs

1 piece char siu

2 stalks green onion

1 small cucumber

1 package kamaboko

3 lettuce leaves

Dressing:

2 Tablespoons sesame seed, toasted

2 Tablespoons sugar

1 teaspoon salt

3 Tablespoons white vinegar

2 Tablespoons shōyu

¼ cup oil

Cut harusame into 3 inch lengths. Cook harusame in hot water for 3 to 4 minutes. Pour into colander, rinse immediately with cold water, and drain. Mix the ingredients for the dressing and set aside. Beat eggs, add a dash of salt, then fry in oil in thin sheets. Let cool and slice into thin 1 inch strips. Slice the remainder of the ingredients into thin 1 inch strips. Put the drained harusame in a bowl. Mix half of the eggs, char siu, kamaboko, vegetables, and dressing with the harusame. Arrange remainder of the vegetables and other ingredients attractively on top of the harusame. Pour rest of the dressing over all, and serve.

PASTA AND NOODLES

This meal was given to us when my second son was born in 1989, hence the recipe name. I have made it many times since, for pot lucks and to give as a meal for friends who have just had a baby. It makes a lot and freezes well. You can prepare the eggplant a day ahead if you want to break up the cooking steps.

–DONNA HIRAGA STEPHENS

Daniel's Eggplant Casserole

        1 16-ounce package mostaccioli or other tube pasta
        3 pounds of eggplant, peeled and sliced ¼ inch thick
        1 cup seasoned flour
     1½ cups olive oil
1 to 2 cups mushrooms, chopped
        1 cup black olives, sliced
        1 onion, chopped
3 to 5 cloves garlic, sliced
     1½ pounds mozzarella cheese, grated
        6 Tablespoons grated Parmesan or Romano cheese
        1 bunch fresh basil or other herbs
        2 jars prepared spaghetti sauce
          Sliced fresh tomatoes for top layer, optional

Preheat oven to 350 degrees. Salt eggplant on both sides and leave for 30 minutes. Sauté garlic, onion, and mushrooms until tender. Mix in olives. Cook pasta according to box instructions, drain, and set aside. Blot excess water from eggplant, then lightly coat eggplant with flour. Brown in olive oil, adding oil as needed until eggplant is soft. Drain on paper towels.

In two layers using a baking dish: Layer sauce (add fresh torn basil pieces with sauce), pasta, eggplant, onions, mushroom, olives mixture, and mozzarella. Repeat layers. Add Parmesan cheese on top with fresh tomato slices. Cover with foil or lid. Bake for 30 minutes. Uncover and bake 10 to 15 minutes. Let stand 10 minutes before serving.

Serves 8 to 10

Fresh Vegetable Pasta

1 pound spaghetti, cooked according to package directions

1 medium onion, chopped

3 garlic cloves, chopped

½ red pepper, chopped

½ green pepper, chopped

1 zucchini, sliced

1 carrot, sliced

2 summer squash, sliced

1 cup broccoli crowns

Vegetable oil for sautéing

1 14-ounce can chopped tomatoes

⅓ cup parsley, chopped

1 cup frozen peas

Salt and pepper to taste

Grated Romano or Parmesan cheese

Steam red and green peppers, zucchini, carrot, squash, and broccoli for about 10 minutes. In large skillet, sauté garlic and onion in olive oil for 2 to 3 minutes. Add steamed vegetables to skillet, along with parsley, peas, salt, and pepper. Stir. Add canned tomatoes and cook for approximately 15 minutes on low heat. Pour half of the sauce over the cooked spaghetti and toss. Divide rest of sauce among individual servings. Sprinkle each serving with grated cheese and serve.

Nabeyaki Udon

  5 cups soup stock (or 5 cups water plus 1 teaspoon hondashi)

¼ cup shōyu

  2 teaspoons sugar

  1 teaspoon salt

½ pound chicken breast, sliced into thin strips

  8 stalks watercress, cut into 1½ inch lengths

  4 green onions, cut into 1½ inch lengths

  1 small carrot, sliced

½ small head napa cabbage, sliced

  3 pieces shiitake, soaked in water for 10 minutes and sliced into strips

½ cake kamaboko, sliced

½ block tōfu, cubed

14 ounce udon, boiled "al dente"

In skillet or pot, combine broth, shōyu, sugar, and salt. Bring to a boil. Add chicken and simmer 5 minutes. Add remaining ingredients (except udon) into separate sections of the skillet or pot and simmer 5 minutes. Do not stir. Add udon to heat. Serve, in individual bowls by placing some udon and arranging other ingredients on top.

Serves 4 to 6

Gon Lo Mein

1 12-ounce package chow mein noodles

1½ Tablespoons oyster sauce

1 teaspoon sesame oil

1 Tablespoon oil

1 small yellow onion, thinly sliced

1 9-ounce package chop suey vegetable mix

2 stalks green onion, cut into 1 inch lengths

½ pound char siu, thinly sliced

2 Tablespoons toasted sesame seeds

Cilantro (Chinese parsley leaves), optional

Sauce:

1 Tablespoon shōyu

½ teaspoon salt

2 Tablespoons oyster sauce

2 teaspoons brown sugar

Dash pepper

Preheat oven to 250 degrees. Place noodles in a 9 x 13 inch baking pan. Add oyster sauce and sesame oil. Mix until the noodles are well coated. Heat the noodles in oven for 10 minutes. Mix the sauce ingredients and set aside. Heat wok or a large skillet. Add oil and coat sides of pan. Stir-fry the yellow onion and chop suey mixture with half the sauce mixture for 2 to 3 minutes. Add the heated noodles and green onions and continue to stir-fry. Add the remaining sauce mixture. Do not overcook. Transfer the noodle mixture to a platter. Stir-fry the char siu in the pan until heated. Sprinkle over the noodles. Sprinkle sesame seeds. Garnish with parsley.

China Meshi

My relatives all had big family banquets at Chinese restaurants, probably because it was cheaper by the head than Nihon shoku. Old-fashioned Chinese restaurants were set up for Chinese family banquets as well, although I suspect that some, like Shanghai Low in San Jose, California, had a largely nikkei clientele because of its location in J-Town. Anyway, the regular restaurant was on the main floor, but upstairs would be one or two floors of banquet space. For a large family gathering, the whole floor was reserved so cousins could run around and play together, while the uncles and aunties circulated from table to table socializing. My dad is about in the middle of ten kids. The oldest, Uncle George, is now 93 and, although nisei, is still more comfortable speaking nihongo. In the early-mid 50s, a whole spate of my older cousins got married. Lots of China meshi! We also used to gather for weddings, funerals, and 61st birthday parties for the men, where they would be ushered into their "second childhood" with a bright red baby hat and bib. All the parties featured speeches, jokes, and entertainment with uncles singing shigin (Japanese poetry) and cousins singing Perry Como songs.

–SHIZUE SEIGEL

Side Dishes

Walnut Chicken Appetizers

3	half chicken breasts, deboned and skinned
½	teaspoon salt
	Dash pepper
1	teaspoon shōyu
1	Tablespoon sherry
2	egg whites
¼	cup cornstarch
1½ to 2	cups walnuts, chopped
	Oil for frying

Cut chicken into bite size pieces. Combine with salt, pepper, shōyu, and sherry. Beat egg whites until foamy. Fold in cornstarch until smooth. Dip chicken into egg whites, then coat with nuts. Fry in hot oil (350 degrees) until golden brown. Drain on paper towels. Serve warm.

Dip in catsup, hot mustard, or sweet and sour sauce, if desired.

Nori Rolls

12	nori sheets, cut in half
1	pound ground pork
1	package kamaboko
1	can water chestnuts
5	shiitake, soaked and sliced, optional
1	egg
2	Tablespoons oyster sauce
6	stalks green onions, chopped
	Pepper to taste
2	teaspoons grated ginger

Mince kamaboko and water chestnuts in food processor. Mix with other ingredients. Put ½ to 2 Tablespoons pork filling into nori sheets. Seal ends with water. Fry in a small pan coated with cooking oil spray.

Kamaboko Tenpura

       2 blocks kamaboko
       1 small can water chestnut
       2 stalks green onions, thinly sliced
12 to 15 medium size shrimps
          Oil for frying

Batter:
    1½ cups flour
     ½ cup water
      2 eggs
      2 teaspoons salt
      2 teaspoons sugar

Grate and chop kamaboko into medium bowl. Add diced water chestnuts and green onions. Add peeled, deveined, and chopped shrimp. Mix batter ingredients in small bowl and add to above ingredients. Drop by teaspoonful into hot oil. Fry until lightly browned.

Clams Obon

       Clams
       Flour to coat
       Salt and pepper to taste
       Parsley, chopped, optional
       Celery seed, to taste, optional
       Garlic salt, to taste, optional
       Oil, to cover rim of shell

Slice clams in half so that each shell will retain half of the meat. Clean the clams as usual, cutting off tough tips of necks. Dip each shell (meat side only) in flour that has been seasoned with salt and pepper with chopped parsley, celery seed or garlic salt. Fry face down in enough hot oil to cover the edges of the shell. Each shell will serve as a little lid. When the floured side is nicely browned, the inside will be nicely steamed. Serve face up. The shell with the crisp clam makes a very attractive serving.

Shrimp/Vegetable Fritters

1 egg
½ cup water
1 cup flour
1 teaspoon baking powder
1 teaspoon salt
1 Tablespoon sugar
½ teaspoon ajinomoto, optional
½ teaspoon black pepper
⅓ cup carrots, slivered
⅓ cup string beans, slivered
½ cup onion, slivered
1 cup shrimp (½ pound), cleaned and finely cut
Oil for deep frying

Add water to beaten egg. Sift dry indgredients together. Add egg to dry ingredients and mix. Add vegetables and shrimp into batter and mix. Drop by tablespoon (small drops are better) in deep fat and fry until golden brown.

Artichoke Dip

   2 14-ounce cans artichoke hearts, sliced or chopped (comes whole in the can)
¾ to 1 cup light sour cream
¾ to 1 cup mayonnaise
¾ to 1 cup Parmesan cheese, shredded
3 to 4 cloves garlic, chopped
      Paprika

Mix all ingredients together, except paprika. Spread mixture into a casserole dish. Sprinkle paprika over the top. Bake at 350 degrees for 20 to 25 minutes or until bubbling and/or it turns brown on top. Can turn oven up to 450 degrees for the last 10 minutes of baking to get the top browned. Serve with bread or crackers.

Satsuma Age (Fish Patties)

5 to 6 pieces fish (crappies or cod)
   1 cup flour
   1 cup water
   ½ cup sugar
1¼ Tablespoons salt
1¼ teaspoons ajinomoto, optional
   ¼ cup goma
   ¼ cup gobo and carrots; peeled, slivered and parboiled for added color and taste
      Oil for frying

Grind fish with a food processor. Add flour, water, sugar, salt, ajinomoto, and goma. Depending on the moisture of the fish, add a little more water. The mixture should have shine and it will be heavy. Mix in gobo and carrots. Using a square of plastic wrap, spray with vegetable oil and form mixture into ½ inch thick patties. Deep fry on medium heat until golden brown.

Homemade Bread

My mother would get up very early in the morning in the winter. She would fire up the stove to warm up the house, then she would make lunches for my father, a couple of boarders, and the children who were in school. She went through three or four loaves of bread each morning. Breakfast was always fried potatoes, bacon or ham, and eggs with toast. She did all of this on a coal stove.

I remember looking wistfully at other school children who, at lunch time, went to the grocery store, and bought a loaf of bread and slices of baloney as their lunch. They were eating "boughten" bread. We had to eat homemade bread, with thick slices of homemade ham!

After 36 years of service on the railroad, my father was fired when World War II erupted. We moved to Salt Lake City. After the war, my mother became very active in the local Buddhist Temple and, for any occasion or at the drop of a hat, she would whip up a batch of homemade bread. They were given to friends and neighbors who were kind to her. This was automatically what she took when she went to see friends whose husbands, wives, or children had passed away.

When the family gets together for holidays and family reunions, we always remember the wonderful bread she used to make. Now my two sisters have taken up the challenge to keep the tradition alive and are baking bread whenever possible, even though the bread maker is available.

The bread won't come out perfect the first time. My sisters say that the flour, yeast, kneading, time, etc., all play a part and it's hard to get it just right at first. My mother used to say that she could feel when the dough was right and would make wonderful bread. My sisters have finally gotten to this point.

—Jeanne Konishi

Grandma Chiyo's Bread

> 1 package yeast
>
> 3 cups warm water
>
> 1 Tablespoon salt
>
> 5 Tablespoons sugar (generous, but not heaping)
>
> 2½ Tablespoons cooking oil

4 to 5 cups flour

Dissolve the yeast in the warm water. Add salt, sugar, oil, and flour, and mix until dough does not stick to your hands. Put dough on a floured board and knead until dough is smooth and elastic (takes from 10 to 15 minutes). Place in a large greased bowl, turning dough once to oil the surface of the dough and prevent it from cracking. Cover with clean dish towel and place in a warm place to rise. You can turn the oven on at its lowest point for a few minutes, turn off, and place dough in oven. When dough has doubled in size, cut into three pieces and shape into loaves. Place in well-oiled loaf pans, making sure the surface of the dough is oiled. Cover and let rise until double in size.

Preheat oven to 350 degrees. Place pans in oven with evenly spaced racks and bake for 40 minutes. (Make adjustments for higher altitudes.) When baked, remove bread from pans, oil the tops of the baked loaves, and let cool. Bread slices more easily if cut the next day.

Yields 3 loaves

Jelly Time Blues

One of the fondest memories of my late mother-in-law, Violet, was how much love, energy, and pride she would put into making guava and lilikoi (passion fruit) jellies in Hawai'i for her church's annual bazaar. Violet's jellies were superb as they were not mass-produced and made store-bought jellies seem second grade. The thought of spreading Violet's jellies on a fresh bagel with cream cheese still makes my mouth water.

The making of jellies was a ritual which began early in the year with the collection of small baby food jars that she would collect, wash, and store. My in-law's garage would have boxes upon boxes filled with these jars and my father-in-law, Dan, would become incensed with the clutter as it would crowd out his golf equipment and make it difficult even to park the car. Nevertheless, he would practice his culturally-conditioned "gaman" and just grumble and mutter under his breath.

Next, came the months of collecting ripe guavas and lilikoi. Members of Violet's church congregation would bring whatever guavas they picked or their friends and families gave them. But they all ended up in my in-law's house where, on a weekly basis, Violet would boil separately the guava and lilikoi fruit and then strain the boiled pulp through cheesecloth. It was quite a task, especially for a lady of her stature and size. Her strength and endurance amazed me and others. Violet made thousands of jars of jelly over the years. Many times, she would bring all the guavas and lilikoi to the church kitchen and cook them there as they had larger pots. The strained liquid would then be frozen and stored in plastic containers and yes, you guessed it, in my in-laws' kitchen and garage refrigerators' freezers. Of course, this would infuriate Dan even more as there was no room for other foods.

continued

All of what has been described so far took place from January through September. However, in October, it was almost full-time jelly making for Violet. It was a joke that she would buy out all of the sugar and pectin on the shelves at Times Supermarket in Kahalu'u's Temple Valley Shopping Center. Daily, the jars were again sterilized in the oven and the strained guava and lilikoi juices were again cooked with just the right amount of sugar and pectin, poured into jars and sealed on top with melted wax. Sometimes the jellies were done at home and at other times at the church's kitchen.

Violet would spend the entire day making jellies and not even have time to cook for her husband. Dan would have to play golf on his own and felt neglected the entire month. Arguments ensued between Dan and Violet. In fact, we would get calls in California from Violet about their arguments. Dan's argument was that Violet promised him that when she retired from Queens Medical Center, they would spend more time together playing golf, something they actually both enjoyed most of the year until October came around.

Finally, when my wife, Ann, finished one of her October long-distance phone calls from her mother, we looked at each other and laughed. How silly, we thought, that this once-a-year ritual could affect the entire family. So we decided to write a song called "Jelly Time Blues" and choreographed a dance in the form of a hula (but not a hula) to the tune. We sang and performed that dance on the Christmas Day 1989, in front of the entire family that was present. We never heard them argue and complain about "Jelly Time" again. The song entitled, "Jelly Time Blues," is sung to the tune of "Crying Time."

–K. Ken Yabusaki

JELLY TIME BLUES

COPYRIGHT 1989 KEN & ANN YABUSAKI
(SUNG TO THE TUNE OF "CRYING TIME")

Oh it's Jelly Time again, oh please don't leave me.
I can see that far away look in your eyes,
I can tell by the way you gather bottles,
that it won't be long before it's Jelly Time.

January, February, March, and April,
May, June, July, August, September are so nice,
But for some reason always come October,
it's time for guava, lilikoi, and Jelly Time.

You said you always wanted to retire
from the gasa gasa times of Church and Queens,
But when I'm golfing all alone at the Pali,
I'm so mad I see the bottle as the ball.

When I come home to you from playing 18 pukas
and I want to show you plenty balls I found,
Instead of ono kau kau on kitchen table,
note says, "Sorry fix own lunch, it's Jelly Time."

I come home from church so tired, hot, and sweaty,
and I see you watching, oh, the damn TV.
I'm so angry I don't want to cook your dinner,
after all it's once a year for Jelly Time.

It's December, Christmas is over, time flies so quickly.
Blood pressures down, humbug, and angers are all pau,
Now they're back together golfing on the Pali,
Enjoy each other now before it's Jelly Time!

Guava Jelly

1 12-ounce can frozen guava juice

6 cups sugar

1 packet pectin

¼ teaspoon butter

6 8-ounce jars

Make juice according to container directions. Strain juice through a cheese cloth into a bowl to make 6 cups strained juice. Mix juice with sugar in a sauce pan and bring to bowl. Add pectin and butter and cook to a fast boil, stirring constantly. As it thickens, check readiness by raising the spoon 12 inches above the pan away from steam. Turn the spoon sideways and let syrup pour off the spoon. When two drops from the spoon come together the jelly is ready. Turn off the heat and skim off the foam. Pour jelly into warmed sterilized jars. Seal with melted paraffin. Makes 5 to 6 8-ounce jars. May be stored on the shelf, but refrigerate once open.

Mango Jam

3 cups mango pulp, mashed

3 cups sugar

2 Tablespoon fresh lemon juice

4 8-ounce jars

Combine ingredients in a sauce pan and boil. Lower heat to medium and cook, stirring constantly approximately 20 minutes. Using warm sterilized jars, pour mixture in and seal with melted paraffin. Makes 4 8-ounce jars. Jam may be stored on the shelf, but refrigerate once open.

Broccoli Casserole

1 bunch fresh broccoli or 2 boxes frozen broccoli

1 cup mayonnaise

1 10.5-ounce can cream of mushroom soup

2 eggs, beaten

1 onion, chopped

Topping:

1 cup grated cheddar cheese, grated

¼ cup margarine, melted

1½ cups bread crumbs

Preheat oven to 350 degrees. Mix broccoli, mayonnaise, soup, eggs, and onion together and put in a 9 x 9 casserole dish (double recipe for 9 x 13 inch casserole). Top with mixture of cheese, margarine, and bread crumbs. Bake for approximately 24 to 30 minutes.

Tamago Maki

6 eggs, beaten

¼ cup dashi (or 1 cup water mixed with 1¼ teaspoon dashi-no-moto)

¾ teaspoon salt

2 Tablespoons sugar

¼ cup frozen peas

1 carrot, peeled, par boiled, and sliced thinly into ¼ inch strips

Small handful of Chinese fungus, soaked in water

Non-stick spray

10 x 10 electric frying pan, heated to 380 degrees

Beat together eggs, dashi, salt, and sugar. Spray frying pan with non-stick spray. Pour egg mixture into the frying pan. Scatter fungus, peas, and carrot strips on top of egg mixture to give color. Cover pan. Check periodically to see if egg mixture is cooked (about 7 to 8 minutes). Flip egg onto cutting board. Place a sudare (coarse bamboo sushi mat) on top of egg. Put another cutting board on top and flip all the layers over so that the cooked egg is on top of the sudare. Roll the egg like a sushi and tie it tightly with string until cool. Refrigerate for about 20 minutes. Cut and serve.

Eggplant Teriyaki

    1 pound Japanese eggplant (4 to 6)
      Sesame oil

Dressing:

    ¼ cup shōyu
    ¼ cup mirin or sake
    ¼ cup sugar
    1 Tablespoon grated ginger
      Toasted sesame seeds

Cut eggplant into 1 inch slices. Soak in water 10 to 15 minutes. Drain and pat dry
with paper towels. Heat large non-stick skillet and add sesame oil ⅛ inch deep.
Cook eggplant slices on both sides until tender, adding more oil as needed.
Remove from heat and drain on paper towel. Arrange eggplant slices in bowl.
Combine shōyu, mirin or sake, sugar, grated ginger, and a few drops of sesame oil.
Pour over eggplant slices and let marinate 10 to 20 minutes before serving.
Sprinkle with sesame seeds.

Warabi

I was walking on the campus at Highline Community College last week when I noticed some warabi so I stopped to pick a handful. I used to cook warabi every spring, but the children did not especially enjoy it. Then, too, my late husband and his buddies were fed a steady diet of salted warabi and salmon when they used to go to Alaska to work in the canneries to raise money for school.

So it was after a hiatus of twenty-some years that I cooked warabi last week. I had forgotten exactly how I used to cook it. I think it was a rather laborious process. The main need is to remove the acid without removing the flavor. I tried the fast method and found it to be quite good. I sautéed my handful and decided to pick some more.

Mid-May is apparently a little late for warabi. Because it has been cold and rainy here in Seattle, there was some still some growing. Then, too, I encountered unfriendly signs that said "Private Property—No Trespassing," but I managed to scrounge around and gather a small boxful.

My next project is to dig up some warabi roots and plant them in a spare garden on my property, hopefully for harvesting the spring of 2000 or 2001.

—Margaret Yanagimachi

Warabi (Fernbrake)

1 large handful warabi

2 teaspoons baking soda

Olive oil for sautéing

Dash sesame oil

Dash of shōyu

Dash of black or red pepper

1 Tablespoon instant dashi

1 clove garlic, chopped, optional

Bacon bits, optional

Pick upper 4 inches of warabi spear. Wash carefully in clear water. Rinse and drain. Cut into 2 inch pieces and return to water. Soak for an hour. Drain. Meanwhile, bring about two quarts or more of water to a brisk boil. Add baking soda. Drop in washed and drained warabi. Blanch for 2 or 3 minutes, while stirring. Drain and soak in clear water for about an hour, changing water two or three times.

Drain thoroughly. At this stage you can package and freeze for later use. Sauté in olive oil and a dash of sesame oil. Season to taste with shōyu and a dash of black or red pepper, and instant dashi. If desired, add chopped garlic or bacon bits.

Potato Casserole

    6 medium potatoes
   ¼ cup butter
    1 can cream of chicken soup
    1 pint sour cream
 1½ cups green onion, chopped
 1½ cup longhorn cheddar cheese, grated

Topping:
    Crushed corn flakes
    2 Tablespoons butter, melted

Cook potatoes in skin until firm; cool, peel, and grate. Preheat oven to 350 degrees. Heat butter and add soup. Blend sour cream, onions, and cheese. Mix in soup. Stir in potatoes and place in buttered casserole. Mix corn flakes with butter and sprinkle on top. Bake for 45 minutes.

Note: If short on time, cook potato the day before and leave skin on to prevent discoloration.

Every summer our garden in Western Massachusetts would overflow with zucchini. My mother would think of all kinds of ways of using it. We had zucchini bread a lot, but our favorite was our mom's zucchini tempura. To her, it was delightful, since there was no zucchini in Japan, but to us, it was just a delicious summer treat: hot and crispy on the outside and soft and sweet on the inside, dipped in homemade tsuyu with fresh grated ginger.

– STEPHEN MURPHY-SHIGEMATSU

Chawan Mushi

2½ cups dashi
½ teaspoon salt
3 eggs, lightly beaten
4 slices kamaboko
8 shrimp, peeled and deveined
3 button mushrooms, thinly sliced
8 sugar snap or snow peas

Mix together the cooled dashi, salt, and eggs. Divide kamaboko, shrimp, mushrooms, and sugar peas among four chawan mushi bowls. Pour the egg mixture in each bowl. Place lid on bowl and place the bowl in a steamer. After the water in the steamer begins to boil, steam for 15 minutes. The custard is done when toothpick inserted into its center comes out clean. Serve immediately.

MAIN DISH

My grandfather, Yetsusaburo Ito, worked as foreman on the Peck family ranch on Sutter's Island in the Sacramento River Delta from 1918 until the beginning of World War II. He and my grandmother, Toku, boarded the seasonal farm workers who, in the early days, were primarily issei men. My grandmother prepared three meals a day for up to 15 workers as well as her own family of 5. She had to produce food in vast quantities and quickly. Luckily, she was an excellent cook, and the lure of her cooking drew workers back year after year. Like most issei women, she did not work from exact recipes, relying on "eye measurement" rather than standard measuring cups or spoons. My mother, Haru, recalls that obāchan made the tallest, fluffiest biscuits in the world, using about "this much" flour, "that much" shortening and milk, and a "little bit" of baking powder, and baking them in a wood-burning iron stove with no temperature control. As in this example, she learned to make many quintessential American dishes and her menus mixed together Japanese and so-called American dishes in one meal, like, for example, chicken stew, rice and tsukemono, or corn beef and cabbage with rice. Also, like other issei, she adapted her cooking to incorporate American foodstuffs into Japanese dishes. Shōyu, sugar, dashi, and ginger could transform just about any meat or vegetable mixture into a Japanese okazu.

The following recipe for eggplant and meatballs is one of her inventions and has been a family favorite for four generations. It is incredibly simple to make and delicious. Preparation of the dish has passed down to me through my mother but without any specific measurements or proportions. This is a rough approximation. The mirin is my own addition—I don't think my grandmother used it. I also experimented with a "healthy" version made with extra lean ground beef, but it lacked the toothsomeness of the original.

– EVELYN NAKANO GLENN

Grandma Ito's Eggplant and Meatballs

1½ pounds eggplant (1 to 2 eggplants)
½ pound ground chuck
1 Tablespoon oil
2 Tablespoons mirin
¼ cup shōyu
2 Tablespoons sugar
¼ cup water

Peel vertical strips of skin off eggplant so that about half of the skin remains. Cut eggplant into 1½ inch cubes. Form hamburger into 1 inch balls. In a large sauce pan, heat oil; brown meat balls in oil, turning over to brown all sides. Cover and steam slightly for 2 to 3 minutes to firm up the balls. Uncover and add mirin, shōyu, sugar, and water; bring to a simmer and loosen any meatballs stuck to the bottom. Add eggplant, turning over contents to get some of the eggplant down toward the bottom, and cover; cook for 7 to 8 minutes, turning over mixture two or three times, until eggplant can be pierced with a fork. Do not overcook. Transfer to a shallow bowl and serve with rice. For an extra treat, spoon some of the eggplanty-hamburgery sauce on top of your rice.

Serves 4 to 6

Pepper Steak Stir Fry

8 ounces beef fillet, frozen
4 Tablespoons shōyu
1 red pepper, sliced
1 green pepper, sliced
2 Tablespoons cooking oil
1 Tablespoon sesame oil
1 Tablespoon hoisin sauce

Thaw frozen meat slightly so it can be sliced ⅛ inch thick. Marinate in shōyu for 1 hour. In hot wok, add 1 Tablespoon oil. Add meat and stir for few minutes until brown. Remove meat, add pepper strips to oil, and stir for 1 minute. Return meat to the wok. Stir in sesame oil and hoisin sauce. Cover and cook for 1 minute. Serve over rice.

Serves 4 to 6

A Bowl of Gohan and Lasagne

My mother comes from a region in Japan that can be compared to the Ozarks of Arkansas. Mom is an inaka girl and her daughter is a little rock n' roll. Mom was raised with the belief that a bowl of gohan and a small dish of tsukemono was a full-course dinner. In America, she was bombarded with images of TV dinners, hotdogs, pasta, Butterball turkeys, aperitifs, appetizers, entrees, side dishes, and dessert. If it was just the two of them, my parents would have survived fine with rice, tsukemono, a vegetable dish, and a Japanese main dish. When my brother and I came along, she realized that our Japanese and American palettes demanded further exploration. After having lasagne at a playmate's house, my brother and I made frequent requests for mom to make it. She had become familiar with ground beef, following our tired whines for burgers like McDonald's.

Mom adapted: spaghetti equaled soba and the tomato sauce replaced the Japanese dipping sauce; pork chops equaled un-breaded tonkatsu; meat replaced fish; canned tuna equaled maguro cooked; and beef stews equaled oden. Mom surprised us one night by making lasagne. She made the basic spaghetti sauce and boiled the wide noodles. She filled a casserole dish with alternate layers of sauce, noodles, sauce, mozzarella cheese, noodles, etc. My brother and I waited anxiously for the lasagne to bake. It was mom's first venture into what we considered gourmet cooking. Mom

continued

scooped up squares of the lasagne as webs of stringy threads of hot mozzarella oozed off the glass Pyrex. My brother and I smiled at each other across the table. Mother began serving our bowls of gohan which always accompanied whatever we had for dinner. We picked up our chopsticks and dove into our squares . . . eagerly anticipating the taste of savory tomato sauce. We knew the wonderful taste would burst into our mouths. Suddenly, my mouth tasted something very odd . . . it was inedible . . . gross. I looked at my brother and he had the same grimace on his face. We both swallowed our bites since spitting it out would have caused an uproar at our dinner table. We attempted to wash out the odd taste with big gulps of milk.

"Mom? The lasagne tastes funny."

"Nani (what)?"

"Ra-za-ni-ya wa chotto okashii (the lasagne tastes a little funny)."

"Nani iutteru no (what are you saying)?"

"It . . . it—it tastes like . . . like . . . like ginger . . . jin-jya no aji suru."

"Soo yo, shōga o iretano ni (Of course it does. I put ginger in it)."

"Mama, doshite (why)? Mama, you don't put shōga in ra-za-ni-ya!"

"Jin-jya, ga-ri-ku (same thing)!"

–Suz H. Takeda

To This Day, I Won't Eat Mutton

Anna Towata recalls her days in Topaz, Utah, mess halls where one of the most served meats was mutton. To this day, Anna will not eat mutton. Who can blame her?

Myself, I love lamb. Here is a recipe that would turn any piece of "mutton" into a dish fit for a king!

–Jo TAKATA

Marinade for Lamb

- 2 racks of lamb
- 1 5-ounce jar Dijon mustard
- 2 Tablespoons shōyu
- 2 cloves garlic, minced
- 1 teaspoon ginger, grated
- 1 teaspoon dry rosemary or 3 Tablespoons fresh rosemary
- 4 Tablespoons olive oil

Mix above ingredients together well, until the consistency of mayonnaise. Trim most of the fat from lamb. Cut down a little between the chops. Brush mixture on the lamb an hour before cooking. Place fat side down and broil about 6 inches away from heat until bubbling and brown, 7 to 8 minutes. Turn racks fat side up and paint with more marinade. Broil until brown and bubbling. Lower pan in the oven. Turn oven to 350 degrees and bake about 20 minutes or more if you like it pink.

Note: You can also use a butterflied leg of lamb. This also works well on a barbeque grill.

Serves 6 to 8

My mother was such a good cook—but she never gave recipes except for "a little of this and a pinch of that." And you never knew what was in the food. We were poor, and she improvised a lot. I can still see her bending over and peering into the refrigerator to see what she could feed us. It was a little unnerving to watch her take out little dishes of leftover food, sniff deeply to make sure it was not tainted, then drop them into the sauce for the noodles, or into the sukiyaki or whatever she was cooking. And yet, not only did they turn out delicious, none of us ever got sick from her cooking!

– Chizu Iiyama

Char Siu

    1 cup sugar

    1 Tablespoon salt

    2 teaspoon saltpeter

    2 teaspoon shōyu

    2 cloves garlic

3 to 4 pounds pork butt

Preheat oven to 350 degrees. Blend first five ingredients. Rub on pork. Slice pork 1 inch to 1¼ inches thick. Let stand three to four hours. Roast 1¾ to 2 hours. If thin, roast one hour.

Beef Mizutaki

1 pound steak

1 block tōfu

1 15-ounce can bamboo shoots

8 large mushrooms

2 packages enoki mushrooms

1 bunch spinach

1 bunch green onions

1 package shirataki

1 chikuwa (cylindrical fishcake)

Creamy Mizutaki Sauce:

2 eggs

1 Tablespoon vinegar

1 cup salad oil

⅔ cup sour cream

4 Tablespoons shōyu

4 Tablespoons mirin

Slice all the ingredients into bite size pieces. Arrange them on a large platter and place it on the table along with an electric frypan. Add water to cover half of pan, boil. Add ingredients in the hot bubbling water, and when all the ingredients are heated through, it is ready for serving.

Creamy Mizutaki Sauce:

Combine the eggs, vinegar and ½ cup oil in a blender until it is creamy. Slowly add the remaining oil, on high speed, until a thin mayonnaise is formed. Add remaining ingredients and mix well. Pour sauce into individual bowls, and dip beef and vegetables from mizutaki. Serve with plain hot rice.

Serves 4

Batā Yaki

½ cube butter (¼ cup olive oil may be substituted, if desired)
½ pound fresh mushrooms, thinly sliced
2 pounds spinach, cut in large pieces
1½ to 2 pounds of flank, sliced very thin on crosswise grain (freeze meat for
     1 hour for easier slicing)

Sauce:

8 Tablespoons daikon (Japanese or Chinese white radish), finely grated
4 Tablespoons fresh lemon juice
4 Tablespoons shōyu
Dash of cayenne pepper

Melt butter in skillet (electric skillet allows table cooking); add mushrooms and sauté. Add spinach and cook until partially done and push to one side. Add beef and sauté briefly. Do not overcook the meat. Mix sauce ingredients together in a bowl. Divide sauce into four portions and place in bowls. Divide bata yaki in four portions. Serve with steamed rice.

Note: Cooked Japanese style, batā yaki is prepared in small batches which are served as more ingredients are cooked. Or you can use a large skillet and prepare all portions at once.

Serves 4

Our Maverick Wine Maker

My dad and mom were immigrant farmers who grew 40 acres of muscat grapes in Reedley, California. These grapes were eaten fresh or dried into raisins. Among the thousands of grapevines were a dozen or so wine grape vines scattered throughout the vineyard—these "maverick" vines were the result of a careless nursery man whose vine cuttings became mixed. Dad was not going to let these wine grapes go unused!

Late in September, he picked them and threw them into a large oak barrel. He crushed them using his bare feet. He did this behind the closed barn doors because he didn't want us kids, all eight of us, to see what he was doing. He, being a faithful Christian of the Methodist denomination, was admonished by the church to refrain from drinking any alcoholic beverage, and making it was certainly a "no no." But we knew what he was doing!

Many months later, the wine occasionally appeared on our dinner table, especially when we had guests. He proudly commented about the beautiful color and fine taste. Of course, the guests would agree and enjoy the creation of our maverick wine maker.

–Lloyd Wake

Kahlbi Kui (Barbecued Short Ribs)

  3 pounds short ribs
3½ Tablespoons brown sugar
  2 teaspoons salt

Marinade:

  ⅓ cup shōyu
1½ Tablespoons brown sugar
1½ Tablespoons sherry
  2 cloves garlic, minced
  2 slices ginger
  2 stalks green onion
  1 Tablespoon toasted sesame seeds
  1 chili pepper
  2 Tablespoons peanut oil

Trim fat from ribs and, if ribs are too thick, split in half. Combine the salt and sugar and rub on ribs. Mash the ginger and mix all marinade ingredients together. Put ribs in a flat pan with the marinade and let stand 1 hour. Broil 7 to 10 minutes. If using charcoal, ribs will be done in 5 minutes over very hot heat.

Serves 6

"Fond Memories of Waikiki"

from the *The Oral History Recorder Newsletter,* Vol. XII, #2, Summer 1995
Social Science Research Institute, University of Hawai'i at Manoa

Helen Kusunoki's parents, Sakazo and Hisako Fujika, raised five children and founded the Unique Lunch Room, a popular Hawai'ian food eatery on the Diamond Head end of Kalakaua Avenue, on the island of Oahu.

"Naturally, Hawai'ian people like to eat their Hawai'ian foods. So, they suggested to my father, why don't he serve Hawai'ian foods? They taught him to make lau-laus (taro leaf-wrapped pork) and things like that. So he started out small, and when people found out that he served Hawai'ian food, the demand got bigger and bigger. That's how he got into the Hawai'ian food restaurant and he changed the name to Unique Lunch Room (instead of Diamond Ice Cream Parlor).

. . . the Hawai'ian boys taught him how to make pipi kaula (beef jerky) the Hawai'ian way, which is you salt it with rock salt and dry it. But the demand was so much, he didn't have time to dry it. He would cut the meat smaller and put o-shōyu and Hawai'ian salt, just a little bit of sugar, and garlic. He would soak that, and then fry it because he didn't have time to dry it. So that was partly Japanese style pipi kaula. But people didn't mind. Because it has that shōyu no aji, ne? Even the haole people liked, you know."

–Helen Kusunoki

Easy Sweet and Sour Spareribs

2 to 4 pounds spareribs, cut to fit pot*
   5 Tablespoons rice vinegar
   5 Tablespoons shōyu
   1 cup water
   ¾ cup granulated sugar
   ½ teaspoon dry mustard
   ½ teaspoon salt
   2 cloves garlic, minced
   1 finger ginger, minced

1½ Tablespoons cornstarch dissolved in 2 Tablespoons water

Put spareribs and all remaining ingredients in large sauce pan and bring to a boil. Cover and lower to a simmer. Continuously remove surface fat. Simmer until fork tender. Thicken sauce with cornstarch and water mixture. Serve sauce over ribs.

* If spareribs are frozen, decrease water and cook as above.

Spareribs

4 to 5 pounds ribs

Sauce:
   1½ cups catsup
   ¾ cup brown sugar
   ½ cup vinegar
   ½ cup honey
   ½ cup shōyu
   1½ teaspoons ground ginger
   ¾ teaspoon ground mustard
   ½ teaspoon garlic powder
   ¼ teaspoon pepper
   1 Tablespoon Worcestershire sauce

Cut ribs into 4 sections and place them meat side up on rack. Cover tightly with foil. Bake at 350 degrees for 1 hour and 15 minutes. Drain oil. Return ribs to pan. Pour sauce over ribs. Bake for uncovered for 35 minutes. Can be grilled on barbeque.

Tōfu and Pork with Bean Sauce

½ pound lean pork, thinly sliced
1 Tablespoon cornstarch
2 Tablespoons shōyu
1 onion, sliced
1 Tablespoon oil
1 rounded Tablespoon black bean sauce (purchased in a jar)
1 Tablespoon sugar
¼ cup water
1 block tōfu
1 teaspoon cornstarch
¼ cup water
2 Tablespoons oyster sauce
2 Tablespoons green onion, thinly sliced

Mix cornstarch, shōyu, and sliced onion. Marinate pork in sauce for ½ hour. Heat wok, add oil and stir fry pork and sliced onion. Mix bean sauce, sugar, and water and add to wok. Cut tōfu into squares. Add to wok and toss lightly. Cover and heat. Mix cornstarch, water, and oyster sauce. Add to wok and mix gently to thicken. Heat and sprinkle with sliced green onion.

Butadōfu

¾ pound pork, cut into bite sized pieces
1 19-ounce carton tōfu, cut into 1 inch cubes
6 green onions, cut into one inch lengths
2 Tablespoons vegetable oil
6 Tablespoons miso
1 piece funyū (fermented bean curd)
½ cup water

Heat oil in skillet and stir fry pork until cooked but not browned. Add tōfu and green onions. Dilute and mix miso and funyū with water and pour evenly over meat and tōfu. Cook over medium heat until tōfu heats through. Stir gently to keep tōfu from crumbling.

Tender Bean Cake Stir Fry

  2 pieces tōfu, cut in small squares

  1 Tablespoon oil

  6 ounce pork meat, very finely chopped

  1 piece garlic, chopped

  1 teaspoon sherry

  1 Tablespoon shōyu

  1 teaspoon sugar

  ½ teaspoon salt

  2 chicken stock cubes mixed with ¾ cup water

  ½ teaspoon cornstarch, mixed with 2 teaspoons cold water

  1 teaspoon sesame oil

    Pinch of red pepper

  2 stalks green onion, cut 1 inch long

Boil tōfu and drain. Set aside. Heat oil and sauté pork meat with chopped garlic until brown. Add tōfu, sherry, shōyu, sugar, salt, and pour in the chicken stock, cover, and simmer for 8 minutes. Stir in cornstarch to thicken sauce and turn off the stove. Before serving sprinkle the sesame oil and red pepper over the dish, then garnish with green onion. Serve with steamed rice.

Spicy Bean Curd

2	packages firm bean curd
2	inch piece fresh ginger, peeled and minced
4 to 5	cloves garlic, peeled and minced
½	pound ground meat (pork, beef, turkey)
2	Tablespoons oil
3	teaspoons prepared Chinese chili-garlic sauce
1	14½-ounce can chicken broth
	Salt and pepper to taste
2 to 3	stalks green onion, chopped
2	Tablespoons shōyu
2	Tablespoons vermouth or rice wine
2	Tablespoons cornstarch
1 to 2	Tablespoons sesame oil

Slice bean curd into ¾ inch squares. Sit in colander to drain until ready to use.

Heat oil; add minced ginger and garlic, and fry lightly. Add the ground meat and fry, stirring to break up lumps. When all the red color is gone, add the chili sauce, and stir to mix. Add the drained bean curd, chicken broth, salt, and pepper. Let the mixture come to a boil and cook over medium heat for 10 to 15 minutes or until bean curd squares look puffed.

Add chopped green onion to bean curd. Mix the shōyu, wine, and cornstarch in a cup until smooth. Pour into the hot bean curd and continue cooking to thicken the sauce. Remove from fire and dribble sesame oil over the dish before serving.

Serve with hot rice and a plain green vegetable for a simple meal or as part of a larger Chinese meal of several dishes.

Vegetarian version: Substitute ¾ cup chopped, cooked or reconstituted mushrooms for meat, and vegetable broth for chicken broth. Dried or fresh shiitake are the best.

Chicken and Rice Fiesta (Arroz Con Pollo)

2½ to 3 pound chicken, cut up
  ¼ cup salad oil
  1 medium green pepper, chopped
  1 medium onion, chopped
  2 cloves garlic, minced
  1 cup uncooked rice
  1 8-ounce can tomato sauce
  1 cup chicken broth
  ½ teaspoon saffron, optional
  2 teaspoons salt
  ¼ teaspoon pepper
  1 8½-ounce can peas, drained with liquid saved

Brown chicken in heavy skillet or electric skillet. Remove chicken and add green pepper, onion, garlic, and rice. Stir occasionally while rice browns. Blend in tomato sauce, chicken broth, saffron, salt, pepper, and liquid from peas. Add the browned chicken. Cover with tight lid and cook over low heat 30 minutes. Remove cover; lift rice with a fork to fluff up. Add peas and cook over low heat about 5 minutes longer. This is an easy, quick and simple chicken and rice dish with a Spanish flavor. If prepared in an electric skillet, it is easily warmed up just before serving.

Optional:
To add a further Spanish flavoring, mix in two links of chorizo (Spanish sausage), sliced, at the same time as the browned chicken.

Serves 4 to 6

CHICK SEXING

The descriptor "chick sexer" today brings a smile to someone who has never heard that term. The chick sexing profession was first developed at the University of Nagoya in Japan in the early 1930s and revolutionized the poultry industry. The early pioneers were trained in chick sexing in Japan, but schools of chick sexing developed in the U.S. One of the main schools was owned by Fred Nitta of Pennsylvania. Many nikkei, early on, dominated this profession. Once the sex of the newly hatched chicks could be determined (by looking at their bottoms) the chicks could be sorted into boxes of pullets or cockerels and shipped by rail while they did not have to be fed. It saved the poultry men and women millions of dollars, and created a highly specialized agricultural profession overnight—one to which the nikkei had special access. Noteworthy also was that it was one of the early specialized professions that allowed nikkei women to become financially independent.

Why were nikkei so good as chick sexers? In addition to the technical skills, when compared to others, the Japanese were quick, efficient, and dead accurate. The hundreds of young issei and kibei men and women who did this work were intelligent, tough, and had unbelievable stamina to go on stretches of 24, sometimes 36, hours without sleep. Their hard work enabled nursery owners, with whom they contracted, beat the competition for high profits.

The season began in December and could drag into early June. It was ferociously intense during the spring months. They were sent throughout the Midwest and Southern states for contract work, sometimes in groups, others singly. Often contracts with nurseryowners stipulated the number of chicks to be processed in an hour and with no less than 98% accuracy!

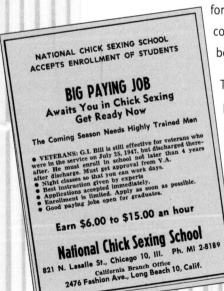

The income was fabulous in those pre-war, and wartime, and early post-war years. Many chick sexers worked 6 months and then gambled 6 months in Nevada. Others were more industrious and quietly built small fortunes. So the next time you hear the words, "chick sexer," don't laugh, as they were among the first of our early pioneers who, through their industrious work, retired early with smiles on their face.

Cheese/Chicken Enchiladas (spicy)

Sauce:

- 4 teaspoons olive oil
- 1 cup yellow onion, chopped
- 2 cloves garlic, minced
- 4 teaspoons chili powder (or more to taste)
- 3 cups tomato puree (2 cans stewed Mexican style tomatoes, pureed)
- 1 cup hot water mixed with 4 envelopes low sodium chicken broth powder
  Pepper to taste
- 2 teaspoons cumin
  Mole sauce, optional (Some brands are very concentrated; add gradually to taste.)

Enchiladas:

- 12 super-sized corn tortillas
- ½ cup green or yellow onion, chopped
- 8 ounces fat-free mozzarella cheese, grated
- 8 ounces reduced fat sharp cheddar cheese, grated

Optional:

- 8 ounces chicken breast, cooked and shredded
- 1 2½-ounce can of sliced olives, drained
  Extra cheese for topping

Preheat oven to 350 degrees. Coat baking pan with vegetable oil spray. In sauce pan, heat oil and sauté onion and garlic until soft. Add chili powder, tomato puree, broth, pepper, cumin, and mole sauce, if used. Stir over heat until well blended. Remove from heat. Heat tortillas in micowave to soften (about 40 seconds on high, 3 at a time). Spread sauce on one side of each tortilla; fill center with equal quantities of onion, cheese, chicken (if used), and dot with olives (if used). Roll tortillas and place side by side in baking pan. Pour remaining sauce over the top. Sprinkle with extra cheese, if desired. Bake about 15 minutes.

Serves 6 to 8

Chicken Mah Fry

   1 fryer chicken, cut into small pieces
    Oil for frying
    Flour for dipping

Marinade:

  ½ cup sugar
  1 teaspoon dried ginger
  1 teaspoon garlic salt
  ½ cup shōyu
  5 cubes funyū (fermented bean curd)
  1 egg

Mix all marinade ingredients together, then marinate chicken for at least an hour. Drain chicken, dip in flour, and fry in deep fat.

Chicken Kawariage

  3 pounds chicken wings
  3 eggs, beaten
   Cornstarch

Sauce:

  1 cup sugar
  ½ cup white vinegar
1½ teaspoons salt
  3 teaspoons water
  3 Tablespoons shōyu

Cut wings into sections. Coat with cornstarch, dip in egg, and fry in about ½ inch oil. Cook sauce on low heat until sugar is dissolved. Place a few wings at a time in sauce and let soak a little while. Place on cookie sheet lined with foil and sprayed with vegetable spray. Bake in 350 degree oven for 15 minutes. Turn over and bake 15 minutes more.

Mom's Almond Chicken

2 whole chickens, cut in half
Salt and pepper to taste
Cornstarch
Oil to fry
Almonds, toasted
Green onions, chopped or slivered

Preheat oven to 375 degrees. Coat chicken halves with salt, pepper, and cornstarch. Fry to golden brown. Place fried chicken halves, skin side down, in oven dish. Pour water in pan (about ½ the depth of the pan) but don't cover the chicken completely. Bake for 1½ hours (45 minutes on each side). Cool. Shred chicken meat and place on big platter. Save juice from pan. Make sauce with pan juices, cornstarch mixed with a little water, salt to taste and shōyu to color, heating until it is a clear brown color. Pour over shredded chicken and garnish with chopped green onions and toasted almonds.

Shōyu Chicken

3 pound fryer chicken
2 cups shōyu
1 cup water
½ cup sugar
1 star anise
1 chunk fresh ginger root, the size of a quarter, crushed
1 stalk green onion, shredded lengthwise and cut in 1 inch lengths

Wash and pat chicken dry. Mix shōyu, water, sugar, star anise, and ginger in a pot which just fits the chicken. Bring shōyu mixture to a boil. Lower chicken into pot and bring back to a boil. Cover. Simmer for 20 minutes. Turn chicken over and simmer for another 20 minutes. Lift chicken out and cool on platter for ½ hour. Rub the chicken with sesame oil then chop into 1 inch by 2 inch pieces and arrange on platter. Pour ¼ cup of the warm sauce over chicken. Garnish with shredded green onion.

Serves 4

Chicken in Wine

8 chicken half breasts

Bisquick

Seasoned salt

1 pound mushrooms

1 onion, chopped

Sauce:

½ cup oil

1 cup white wine

1 clove garlic, crushed (more if desired)

1 teaspoon salt

½ teaspoon pepper

½ teaspoon thyme

½ teaspoon oregano

½ teaspoon rosemary

Preheat oven to 350 degrees. Roll chicken in Bisquick, then sprinkle with seasoned salt. Bake uncovered at 450 degrees for 30 minutes. Sauté onions and mushrooms in a little oil, then mix with sauce. Mix remaining ingredients in sauce pan and simmer. Pour over baked chicken. Cover and bake for 45 minutes.

Serves 4 to 6

Sweet and Sour Peanut Chicken

8 to 10 chicken breasts

  ½ teaspoon salt

  ½ cup flour

  2 eggs

  1 cup panko (Japanese bread crumbs)

    Oil

  1 head lettuce

  2 bunches green onions

  ½ cup chopped peanuts

Sweet and Sour Sauce:

  2 cups chicken stock

  3 Tablespoons vinegar

  1 cup sugar

  ¾ cup catsup

  1 clove garlic

    Cornstarch mixed with cold water to thicken

Skin and debone the chicken breasts. Sprinkle salt on them evenly. Beat eggs. Dip chicken in the flour, then the eggs, and then the panko.

Heat oil in skillet. Over medium heat, put breasts in skillet; allow to brown on one side before turning. The chicken breasts should be completely cooked. Transfer onto paper towels. When chicken is cooled, slice each into ¾ inch pieces. Keep each breast together.

Slice up lettuce to lay the chicken breasts on. Simmer all sauce ingredients together in a pot. Pour over chicken. Top chicken with green onions and chopped peanuts.

Serves 4 to 6

Mom's Fried Chicken

Mom always fried chicken for church and JACL potlucks and family gatherings, a good enticement for us kids to attend. The lingering smell is etched in my memory; good food and love shared with many. Each of us learned how to make this dish, and Mom still offers advice: "The oil must be hot enough so that the chicken sizzles when you dip it in the sauce. Don't soak it, just dip it!" My sisters will add, "More garlic!" and "More ginger!"

The origins of this family recipe are unclear. Mom says she got it from Auntie Juen Oishi who may have gotten it from her sister-in-law, Aki Toriyama. But Auntie Juen can't confirm this. Others in the family think the recipe belonged to Mori-san, Uncle Masao Mori, who must have created delicious memories in his home years ago with this chicken.

Anyway, I treasure the many good times we've shared and I love Mom's fried chicken.

–Marion Oishi Suzuki

Mom's Southern Fried Teriyaki Chicken

> 1 fryer chicken, cut up into small pieces
> 1 egg
> Flour

Sauce:
> ½ cup shōyu
> ½ cup dry sherry, sauterne, or mirin, optional
> ¼ cup sugar
> 1 clove garlic (or more), minced
> 1 piece ginger, grated

Coat chicken first with beaten egg, then flour. Deep fry 10 minutes until lightly browned. Mix sauce ingredients in a bowl. While sizzling hot, dip one at a time in sauce. Place in casserole or baking pan. Bake at 250 to 275 degrees for 15 to 30 minutes or until done.

Honey Chicken Wings

    3 pounds chicken wings
    1 cup honey
    ½ cup shōyu
    2 Tablespoons catsup
    1 clove garlic (or more), chopped

Cut off and discard wing tips. Cut each wing into 2 parts. Combine remaining ingredients and mix well. Place wings in slow cooker (crock pot) and pour sauce over. Cook all day on low setting.

Serves 4 to 6

Mochiko Chicken

3 to 5 pound chicken thighs, deboned and cut in finger size pieces
    Oil for frying
    2 Tablespoons flour
    ¼ cup cornstarch
    ¼ cup mochiko
    ¼ cup sugar
    2 Tablespoons green onions, minced
    1 clove garlic, minced
    2 teaspoons salt
    ¼ cup shōyu
    1 Tablespoon oyster sauce
    2 eggs, beaten
    1 Tablespoon sesame oil
2 to 3 chili peppers, minced, optional

Combine all ingredients except oil for frying. Add chicken and marinate two hours or longer; overnight for a tastier dish. Cover frying surface of skillet with oil, brown and cook chicken on both sides until done.

Baked Chicken

1 chicken, cut up
1 cup fine bread crumbs
½ cup Parmesan cheese, grated
⅓ pound butter or margarine
Waxed paper

Preheat oven to 325 degrees. Mix bread crumbs and cheese. Melt butter. Dip pieces of chicken in melted butter. Roll in bread crumb mixture. Wrap in wax paper. Place in baking pan with wax paper ends under chicken. Bake for 45 minutes until wax paper is brown.

Chicken Cacciatore

2 pound fryer chicken
½ cup enriched flour
1 teaspoon salt
⅛ teaspoon pepper
2 cups cooking oil
1 clove garlic, minced
1 small onion, sliced
1 8-ounce can tomato paste
2 cups water
½ cup green bell peppers, minced
1 4-ounce can mushrooms
¼ teaspoon allspice
½ teaspoon ground oregano
2 teaspoons salt
¼ cup red wine, optional

Coat chicken with flour, salt, and pepper. Brown in hot oil. Remove from pan. In same oil, sauté garlic and onions. Add tomato paste, water, green pepper, mushrooms, and seasonings. Add chicken. Cover and simmer over low heat about 45 minutes or until chicken is tender. If adding wine, cook 5 minutes longer then remove from heat. Serve with spaghetti noodles.

Kalua Turkey

1 14 or 15 pound turkey, roasted
1 35-fluid ounce bottle liquid smoke
1 can 7-Up
   Hawai'ian salt

Bake turkey and shred. Pour liquid smoke over the meat, little by little. Pour a ½ can 7-Up and taste; use additional 7-Up as needed. Sprinkle Hawai'ian salt to taste. Put in baking pan. Cover with foil and bake at 350 degrees for 30 to 45 minutes.

Chicken Katsu

5 pounds chicken thighs, boneless and skinless
2 eggs, beaten with a little water
   Flour
   Panko
   Oil for frying

Marinade:

1 Tablespoon mirin
⅔ cup shōyu
2 Tablespoons flour
2 Tablespoons sugar
4 pieces garlic, crushed
1 piece ginger, crushed
   Dash salt

Tonkatsu sauce:

½ cup catsup
2 Tablespoons Worcestershire sauce
½ teaspoon dry mustard, mixed with a little water

Marinate chicken thighs several hours or overnight. Flour each piece of chicken. Dip in mixture of eggs beaten with a little water. Dip in panko and deep fry. Mix sauce ingredients together. Serve in bowl with chicken or pour over platter.

Pressed Mandarin Duck

- 1 medium size dressed duckling
- 3 stalks green onions
- 2 stalks celery

Marinade:

- 1 teaspoon salt
- ¼ cup shōyu
- 1 teaspoon sugar
- 2 Tablespoons vegetable oil

Sweet and sour sauce:

- ½ cup white vinegar
- ½ cup sugar
- ½ cup pineapple juice
- ¼ cup catsup
- 1 teaspoon Worcestershire sauce
  Cornstarch mixed with a little cold water
- 4 drops hot sauce, optional
  Almonds, toasted and finely chopped

Place duck in a large pan. Mix marinade ingredients and rub all over the duck. Pour the remainder of the marinade into the cavity, swishing it around until cavity is drenched. Drain. Place duck on a dish and place green onions and celery over the duck. Place duck in a pot and steam, covered, for 2½ hours. Remove and, when cool to handle, remove all bones, making sure that the original shape of the duck is not disturbed.

Place the boned duck on a large platter and press down to ¾ inch thickness with hands. Sprinkle generously with cornstarch on both sides of the duck. Steam platter in a roast pan for 30 minutes. In a deep frying pan, heat oil. Cut the steamed, pressed duck into quarters. Deep fry each quarter in hot oil until golden brown. Remove with strainer and drain on paper towels. Add oil as needed to fry all pieces. With a cleaver, slice duck into 1½ x 1½ inch pieces. Line serving platter with sliced lettuce; arrange duck pieces on lettuce.

Prepare the sweet and sour sauce by mixing all sauce ingredients except cornstarch. Heat until boiling. Then thicken with cornstarch, stirring until medium thick. Top with sweet and sour sauce and garnish with finely chopped toasted almonds. Serve with hot rice.

Tuna with Honey Onion Compote

4 pieces tuna steaks

Salt to taste

4 Tablespoons olive oil

1 teaspoon thyme

¼ teaspoon red-pepper flakes

4 red onions, peeled and thinly sliced

2 Tablespoons red wine vinegar

1 whole clove garlic

¼ teaspoon Tabasco

2 Tablespoon capers, drained

2 Tablespoon honey

2 teaspoons pepper

2 Tablespoons fresh basil, chopped

Preheat the broiler. Cut out dark meat on the tuna. Brush with olive oil and sprinkle with thyme and pepper flakes. Wrap with plastic and let sit for 15 minutes.

Using a large pan, heat the leftover olive oil and add onions. Cover and cook for 15 minutes over medium heat stirring occasionally. Onions can be cooked over higher heat if desired. When the onions brown, uncover and add the vinegar, garlic and tabasco. Add salt to taste. Cook and stir until the vinegar has almost evaporated. Stir in the capers and honey. Cover and simmer for 15 minutes. Onions should be somewhat carmelized.

Unwrap the tuna and sprinkle with pepper and salt. Place fish on a broiler pan 4 inches away from flame. Fish broils quickly, 3 minutes for each side. When done serve tuna with a sprinkle of basil and onion compote. Tuna may also be grilled.

Serves 4

This is an incredibly simple dish, but a real treat. It is best when the freshest fish is used and the seasonings are minimal. Grandpa used to especially enjoy the flesh around the eyes and cheeks of the fish.

– Midori Yenari

Broiled Louisiana Gulf Fish

1 lean fish, with white flesh is best such as flounder, red fish, or trout
Salt and pepper to taste
Daikon, finely grated
Shōyu

The fish should be cleaned, but the head and bones can remain. Preheat broiling pan in oven. Lightly salt and pepper fish. Broil skin side up (do not try to turn over, otherwise the fish might fall apart) for no more than 5 minutes. The fish is ready when the flesh turns white. Do not over broil! Serve with shōyu or daikon oroshi mixed with shōyu.

Steamed Fish

1 rock cod or mullet (1½ to 2 pounds), scaled and cleaned
½ teaspoon salt
1 small yellow onion, sliced
½ cup of 1 inch slices of green onion
1 lemon, sliced
2 shiitake, softened in water and slivered

Sauce:
2 Tablespoons shōyu
¼ teaspoon fresh ginger, grated

Garnish:
Cilantro, leaves only
Green onion, chopped

Salt fish inside and out. Place on heat resistant platter and arrange onion, green onion, lemon, and shiitake on the fish. Place fish platter in large pot with at least ½ inch of water on bottom. Steam for 20 to 25 minutes or until meat is flaky. Garnish with cilantro leaves or green onions. Serve with sauce.

Serves 4

Shellfish Cioppino

Sauce:

- 1 large onion, chopped
- 1 bunch green onions, sliced
- 1 green pepper, diced
- 2 whole cloves garlic, slightly crushed
- ⅓ cup olive oil
- ⅓ cup parsley, chopped
- 2 15-ounce cans tomato puree
- 2 8-ounce cans tomato sauce
- 1 cup white or red wine
- 2 cups water
- 1 bay leaf
- 1 Tablespoon salt
- ¼ teaspoon pepper
- ⅛ teaspoon rosemary
- ⅛ teaspoon thyme

- 3 medium crabs, cleaned and cracked
- 2 dozen clams, scrubbed clean
- 1 pound prawns

Sauté the first 5 ingredients for 5 minutes. Add the rest of the ingredients, except shellfish. Simmer sauce for 1 hour. Remove the garlic. In a large pot, layer the crabs and clams. Pour the hot sauce over the shellfish, cover pot, and bring to a boil. Lower heat and cook for 15 minutes. Add the prawns and cook for another 5 minutes until the clams have opened. Serves 6.

Hint: Sauce may be made several days in advance and reheated before adding to the shellfish. Fish and calamari may be added.

Quick and Easy Nabemono

      2 teaspoons dashi
      2 cups water
      1 can chicken broth
3 to 4 king crab legs, chopped in 1½ inch lengths
      ½ pound fresh shrimp, cleaned
      ½ pound scallops
      1 block tōfu, cut into about 1 inch cubes
      1 15-ounce can shirataki noodles
      6 ounces fresh mushrooms or 1 package enoki mushrooms
        Napa cabbage, cut in 1½ inch lengths
        Green onions, cut in 1½ inch lengths
        Ponzu dipping sauce
        Daikon, grated

Boil water with dashi in a table top cookware or on stove. Add chicken broth. When broth begins to boil, add shirataki noodles and seafood. As ingredients start to boil, add vegetables and tōfu. Cook 2 to 3 minutes or until desired doneness. Serve with ponzu dipping sauce and grated daikon.

Note: ½ pound thinly sliced chicken or ½ pound thinly sliced beef may be used in place of a seafood.

Honolulu Boat Builder

BY USABURO KATAMOTO

from the *Oral History Recorder Newsletter,* Vol. XIII, #3, Fall 1996
Social Science Research Institute, University of Hawaiʻi at Manoa

Japanese in Kakaʻako area were mostly fishermen. They come from mostly Yamaguchi, Hiroshima prefecture and those days the fishermen fell into different categories. One type goes after ahi (yellow-fin tuna). And, there's another type fishermen, aim for aku (shipjack) only . . .

Every week's catch, they divide the money. They take sixty percent for crew and forty percent for boat owners. Crew pays their food expenses during the fishing week. And both got to look after the boat expenses.

Hawai'i Style Oden Stew

8 cups fish broth or stock

½ cup shaved bonito flakes

1 to 2 cups tied konbu

1 to 2 large daikon (white radish)

2 potatoes

6 fried fish cakes

1 to 2 fried tōfu cakes

2 8-ounce cans bamboo shoots

Seasoning:

1 Tablespoon sugar

½ teaspoon salt

1 Tablespoon shōyu

Sake for taste, optional

Chopped green onions for garnish

Soften the konbu separately in 2 cups of broth for about 15 to 20 minutes. Set aside. Heat the remaining broth in a large pot. Clean and cut daikon in ½ inch thick pieces and add to broth. Cook daikon until partly soft, about 10 to 15 minutes, on medium heat. Add konbu and liquid to broth. Boil. Peel and boil potatoes separately. Drain potatoes and set aside. Cut fish cake (different types okay) in diagonal pieces and the tōfu in squares. Add to broth, then add bamboo shoots. Bring to boil for about 10 to 15 minutes. Add bonito flakes and cook for about 5 minutes on low heat. Put in seasoning. Finally, include potatoes and continue cooking for a few more minutes. Add seasoning. Cool, then refrigerate. Best served the next day, reheated, with green onion garnish.

Serves 5

Flashback: Pacific Mercantile, Denver, Colorado

The Pacific Mercantile today exists as a modern cornucopia of foodstuffs catering to a Pan-Asian population. The distinct smells still come back to me: the bamboo casks filled with rakkyo, umeboshi, and beni shōga; the old wooden floors; and the ever-present pungent odor of fish.

I put in time at the Pacific Mercantile as a teenager, working as a stockboy. The store was owned by Mr. Y. Inai. His sons, Robert and Sam, helped out, along with his daughter Susie and her husband, Roy Nagai. My dad said the Inais were running the store since before the war. I thought they had been there a lot longer because everyone looked old to me.

New Year's was the biggest time of the year at Pacific. I never saw so much rice sold, mochi being made, or tōfu delivered. I never saw so much fish cake: kamaboku, chikuwa, char siu, tenpura, and even more fancy fish cake. I remember one that had a flower on each slice. Everyone wanted an Ise Ebi for the New Year table, the longer the antennae the better. That was alright by me because the Ise Ebi with the broken antennae ended up for lunch in the back room.

During the Christmas break we would hire a lot of the college students who were home for the holidays. Somehow they could not quite get the knack of scaling a hundred pound sea bass or calculating how many cans of sekihan went on a particular shelf. The new crop rice had to be stored in the small store rooms in the back of the store and new canned goods—from trading companies like Nishimoto Trading, Japan Foods, and North American—had to be shelved.

Like many general stores, the Pacific was a place to meet and socialize. All the old issei men came to pay their respects to Mr. Inai. I was always told that the Japanese I heard was the "wrong" kind. I would always hear the old men say "Ooi, dō ka?" or "genki?" There would be lots of laughter and nihongo spoken. I felt a part of all this, even though I couldn't quite understand all that was going on.

It gave me a feeling of home; sometimes I still miss it.

— Donald Yamamoto

DESSERTS

Apple Dumpling

Crust:

- 1 cup butter
- 1 cup sugar
- 2 eggs
- 1 Tablespoon milk
- 1 teaspoon baking powder
- 3 cups flour
- 1 teaspoon vanilla

Filling:

- 2½ pounds (8 cups) cooking apples, peeled, quartered, cored, thinly sliced
- ⅓ cup firmly packed light brown sugar
- ⅓ cup granulated sugar
- 1 Tablespoon cornstarch or 2½ Tablespoons flour
- 1 teaspoon cinnamon
- ¼ teaspoon ground nutmeg
- ¼ teaspoon salt
- 2 Tablespoons butter

Preheat oven to 350 degrees. Cream butter and sugar; add eggs, milk, dry ingredients, and vanilla. Put aside ¼ of the dough. Spread rest of dough on bottom and sides of 9 x 13 inch pan. Spread filling over dough.

Place apples in a large bowl. Mix sugars, cornstarch, cinnamon, nutmeg, and salt in a small bowl; sprinkle over apples. Toss gently to mix. Let stand until a little juice forms, about 10 minutes. Pile apple mixture into pastry and dot with butter.

Crisscross rest of the dough over the filling. Dough is soft but lattice strips can be done roughly. Bake for 45–50 minutes until crust is golden.

Auntie Uki Dango

3 cups flour

3 teaspoons baking powder

3 eggs

Pinch of salt

2 Tablespoons black sesame seeds

½ cup evaporated milk

½ cup water

1 cup sugar

1 Tablespoon oil

Oil for deep frying

Mix all ingredients. Deep fry by dropping teaspoon size dough into hot oil. Adjust heat to ensure even cooking of dough into golden brown balls.

Sembei with Mochiko

4 cups flour

1 cup mochiko

3 teaspoons baking powder

1 teaspoon salt

3 Tablespoons sugar

2 Tablespoons black goma

1¼ to 1⅔ cups water

Oil for frying

½ cup shōyu

½ cup sugar

Mix the first 6 dry ingredients, adding water gradually until dough is heavy. Let rest for 20 minutes. Roll dough into thin layer and cut into desired shape. Fry until crisp. Boil shōyu and sugar in a saucepan, then cool slightly. Pour over the fried sembi. Mix well. Spread out on a cookie sheet and dry in a 200 degree oven.

"Sweet Tooth" Nellie Takeda recalls that, as a young girl in Alameda, the highlight of her week was to go to the movies on Sunday afternoons after church. Remember that during the 1920s, most Japanese children attended Japanese school after regular school and on Saturdays, too! Papa would give her a dime for the movie and popcorn but, to her, that wasn't enough. Nellie and her friends would get a long stick and wrap gum around one end. On their way to the movie, they would put the stick in the grates along the gutters hoping to retrieve coins that people had dropped! This way they would be able to buy another treat!

– Jo TAKATA

No Fail Toffee

1⅓ cups whole almonds
½ cup butter
¾ cup light brown sugar, medium packed
⅔ cup chocolate chips

Place almonds on a sheet in a 400 degree oven and bake for 12 to 14 minutes, stirring occasionally. After cooled, place one cup of almonds on a baking sheet. Nuts should be touching. In a small heavy saucepan, slowly melt butter. Set timer for exactly 6 minutes. Drop brown sugar into the butter and stir constantly on medium heat for exactly 6 minutes. Quickly pour mixture over prepared nuts and spread to cover almonds. While toffee is still hot, sprinkle with chocolate chips and spread to cover. Coarsely chop remaining ⅓ cup of almonds. Sprinkle chopped almonds over chocolate. Cool. Break into pieces and enjoy!!

Heath Bar Candy

  1 cup brown sugar
  1 cup butter
    Saltine crackers
  1 package milk chocolate morsels

Preheat oven to 325 degrees. Melt brown sugar and butter over low heat to a boil. Boil for 3 to 4 minutes. Line cookie sheet with crackers. Pour brown sugar and butter mixture over crackers. Bake for 15 minutes and immediately spread chocolate morsels on top. As morsels melt, spread with knife. Refrigerate. When hard, break into pieces. Keep in refrigerator.

Japanese Party Mix

  2 12-ounce boxes Crispix cereal
  2 cups Kix cereal
  ½ cube butter
  ¼ cup oil
  ¼ cup corn syrup
  ¼ cup sugar
  1 Tablespoon shōyu
  1 bottle furikake, without fish

Preheat oven to 250 degrees. Heat butter, oil, corn syrup, sugar, and shōyu in a pan. Pour over cereal and mix well. Sprinkle furikake over cereal. Spread out on cookie sheet and bake for one hour, stirring every 15 minutes. Turn out on waxed paper to cool.

Mandarin Orange Jello with Sherbet

1 3-ounce package orange Jello

1 cup boiling water

1 cup orange sherbet

1 11-ounce can mandarin oranges, drained

Add boiling water to jello. Stir until completely dissolved. Fold in orange sherbet and mandarin oranges. Refrigerate to set.

Jello Mousse

1 6-ounce package apricot Jello

2 cups water

1 20-ounce can crushed pineapple

1 8-ounce package cream cheese, thoroughly mashed

1 8-ounce tub Cool Whip

Combine Jello, water, and pineapple in a small sauce pan. Bring to a boil and cool. Combine cream cheese and Cool Whip. Add this mixture to jello and pineapple. Pour into mold or bowl and refrigerate.

Note: Do not use non-fat products as the mixture will not gel.

Rainbow Finger Jello

First Layer:

 2 envelopes Knox gelatin

 ½ cup cold water

 1 6-ounce package Jello

 1 cup boiling water

 1 cup cold water

Second layer:

 2 envelopes Knox gelatin

 ½ cup cold water

 1 cup boiling water

 1 14-ounce can sweetened condensed milk

 1 cup cold water

Third layer:

 2 envelopes Knox gelatin

 ½ cup cold water

 1 6-ounce package Jello, different flavor than first layer

 1 cup boiling water

 1 cup cold water

Lightly grease (corn oil cooking spray works well) a 9 x 13 inch pan.

First layer:

In a small bowl, mix Knox gelatin with ½ cold water until dissolved. In a separate bowl, thoroughly mix Jello with 1 cup boiling water until Jello dissolves. Add in Knox gelatin; stir in until well blended. Add 1 cup cold water; stir thoroughly. Pour into pan. Refrigerate on a flat surface for about 20 to 30 minutes.

Second layer:

While first is refrigerating, dissolve Knox gelatin in ½ cup cold water in small mixing bowl. Add in remaining ingredients in order given, mixing well after each addition. Cool at room temperature.

After 20 minutes, check refrigerated Jello; it should be firm enough to jiggle and leave fingerprints when touched, but not yet at a hard set. When Jello reaches this soft/firm stage, gently ladle condensed milk mixture over first layer. If it runs into the Jello put pan back in refrigerator for a firmer set. *Note:* Don't let Jello get too hard, otherwise cream layer will slip off when cut. Refrigerate both layers for an additional 20 to 30 minutes.

Third layer:

Repeating instructions for first layer, but using a different color of Jello. Condensed milk layer should also be at a soft/firm set before ladling in third layer. Refrigerate until entire pan is hard set; cut into small squares and serve.

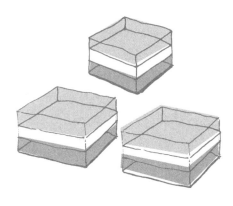

Mom's lemon pie is a family favorite, and you know it's a special occasion when she bakes it. I'm writing this story for my mom because she's too modest to tell you that no one in the family even dares to make lemon meringue pie because no one else's recipe or attempt can even come close to Mom's in flavor, color, and texture. I'm not sure whether the title of this recipe means that this ever won a prize, but it should have. It is simply the best! Even though the rest of us don't have Mom's special touch, this recipe will get you very close to her specialty.

– MAUREEN IWAHASHI KAWAOKA

Pie Crust (for 2 10-inch pie shells)

2¾ cups all-purpose flour
¾ cup Crisco
1 teaspoon sugar
1 teaspoon baking powder
¾ teaspoon salt
⅓ cup ice cold water

Sift dry ingredients together. Cut shortening into flour until it is pea size. Add ice cold water, a tablespoon at a time, until dough holds together. Gather dough into large ball, then divide into two balls. Refrigerate for 10 to 15 minutes.

Liberally dust board or working surface with flour; also rolling pin. Evenly roll out dough into large circle until it is 1 inch larger than pie pan. Fit into pan. Flute edges. Prick bottom and sides with fork. Place a smaller pie pan on top of prepared crust and bake in 400 degree oven for 10 minutes. Remove smaller pie pan and continue baking crust for another 10 to 15 minutes in 300 degree oven until golden brown. Cool.

Prize Lemon Pie

    1 baked 8-inch pie shell
    4 eggs, separated (2 egg whites each in 2 separate bowls)
    ¾ cup sugar
    3 Tablespoons sugar for meringue
    4 level Tablespoons cornstarch
    4 Tablespoons lemon juice
    1 teaspoon lemon juice for meringue
    1 cup boiling water
    1 Tablespoon butter
    1 lemon rind, grated

Beat egg yolks. Add sugar mixed with cornstarch, then lemon juice. Continue beating until light. Put water, butter, and grated lemon rind in top of double boiler; place over simmering water in bottom pot. Heat mixture until butter is melted and mixture heated to near boil. Add egg mixture slowly, stirring constantly until thick. Beat two egg whites until stiff. Fold into lemon custard. Pour into baked pie shell.

Preheat oven to 400 degrees. Beat remaining 2 egg whites with 1 teaspoon lemon juice until fluffy. Gradually add 3 Tablespoons sugar, beating until stiff peaks form. Top pie with meringue, sealing edges to crust. Brown in oven until golden.

Note: For pot lucks, triple recipe and bake in 2 10-inch pie shells or in a 19½ x 15½ inch jelly roll pan using this alternate crust:

    1 cup butter or margarine
    2 cups flour
    ⅓ cup powdered sugar
    1 egg yolk

Combine flour and sugar in bowl. Cut in butter until mixture is the texture of fine crumbs. Work in egg yolk with hands to make pliable dough. Spread into jelly roll pan with fingertips. Bake at 350 degrees for 20 to 25 minutes until light brown.

Summer Fruit Tart

Crust:

 1 cup flour
 ½ cup butter or margarine
 ½ cup powdered sugar

Cream Filling:

 ½ cup whipping cream
 1 8-ounce package cream cheese, softened
 ⅓ cup sugar
 2 teaspoons dark rum or orange juice
 1 teaspoon vanilla
 ¼ teaspoon almond extract

Fruit Topping and Glaze:

2 to 4 medium peaches (or nectarines), peeled, pitted, thinly sliced
 Any fruit in season to add color for garnish
 1 Tablespoon lemon juice
 Marie's Peach Glaze or homemade*

Preheat oven to 350 degrees. In a food processor or medium bowl, combine flour and sugar. Whirl margarine in or cut in with 2 knives. Press dough with hands or with spoon over bottom and 1 inch up the sides of a 9 inch tart pan with removable bottom. Bake in oven for 25 to 35 minutes until golden brown. Cool as you prepare filling and topping. You can cover and chill up to a day.

Chill a medium mixing bowl and beaters of an electonic mixer. Whip ½ cup whipping cream until soft peaks form. Set aside. In a small bowl, beat cream cheese with sugar until fluffy. Add rum or orange juice, vanilla, and almond extract; beat until smooth. Gently fold in whipped cream with spatula. Turn mixture into cooled crust; spread evenly. Cover and chill for 2 to 4 hours.

Before serving, toss sliced fruit with lemon juice to prevent fruit from browning. Arrange slices of fruit, overlapping in a circular pattern over the filling. Brush or spoon glaze over the fruit.

Remove sides of tart pan; transfer to a serving platter. Cut into wedges to serve.

Serves 10 to 12

Homemade Peach Glaze:

Melt ¼ cup peach preserves with 2 teaspoons honey over low heat. Add a squeeze of lemon. Remove any large pieces of fruit or strain. Another way to make a fresh fruit glaze is to strain ½ cup juice from mashed fruit (water can be added), and add to a mixture of 1 Tablespoon cornstarch and ⅓ cup sugar. Cook and stir until thick and clear over medium heat. Add 1 teaspoon lemon juice. Cool.

Honey Fruit Pizza

Crust:

- ½ cup butter or margarine, softened
- ¾ cup sugar
- 1 egg
- 1½ cup flour
- 1 teaspoon cream of tartar
- ½ teaspoon baking soda

Filling:

- 1 8-ounce package cream cheese, softened
- ¼ cup honey
- Fresh fruit, sliced

Preheat oven to 400 degrees. Mix together the butter and sugar. Add egg and mix well. Stir in the flour, cream of tartar, and baking soda. Spread in a greased 14 inch pizza pan. Bake for 10 to 12 minutes or until it begins to brown. Cool. Mix the cream cheese and the honey together. Spread on cooled crust. Top with sliced fruit of choice.

Mango Chiffon

1 packet unflavored gelatin
¼ cup water
4 eggs, separated
1 cup mango pulp, mashed
1 cup sugar
¼ cup lemon juice
Dash salt
1 baked 9 inch shell

Soften gelatin in water. Beat egg yolks well and add to gelatin. Beat in mango pulp and ½ cup sugar. In a sauce pan, cook mango mixture over low heat. Cool slightly. Stir in lemon juice. Chill until mixture begins to thicken. Beat egg whites and salt until soft peaks form. Gradually add remaining ½ cup sugar until stiff peaks form. Gently fold in mango mixture. Pour into pie shell and chill until firm. If desired top with sweetened whipped cream and sliced mangoes.

Serves 8

Chocolate Chip Cake

1 package chocolate fudge cake mix
1 3-ounce small package chocolate pudding mix
1 cup sour cream
4 eggs
½ cup warm water
½ cup oil
3 Tablespoons melted butter
1 12-ounce package chocolate chips

Preheat oven to 350 degrees. Mix all ingredients except chocolate chips with mixer. Fold in chips. Pour batter in a bundt pan or a 9 x 13 inch pan. Bake for 50 to 60 minutes.

Banana Chiffon Cake

- 2¼ cups cake flour
- 1½ cups sugar
- 3 teaspoons baking powder
- 1 teaspoon salt
- ½ cup cooking oil
- 5 egg yolks, unbeaten
- ⅓ cup water
- 1 cup ripe banana, mashed
- 1 teaspoon vanilla
- 1 cup egg whites (7 to 8 eggs)
- ½ teaspoon cream of tartar

Preheat oven to 325 degrees. Sift together flour, sugar, baking powder, and salt into a bowl. Make a well in the flour and add oil, eggs yolks, water, banana, and vanilla. Beat mixture until smooth. In a large mixing bowl, beat egg whites and cream of tartar for about 5 to 7 minutes until stiff. Pour the flour mixture into the egg white mixture, gently folding with a spatula, until just blended. Pour into a 10 inch tube pan. Bake for 55 minutes. Raise heat to 350 degrees and bake for 10 to 15 minutes. Insert a thin skewer to test for doneness. Skewer should come out clean. Invert cake on cans and let rest until cool. Frost with whipped cream.

Fruit Cocktail Pudding Cake

    2 cups flour
    2 teaspoons baking soda
    ½ teaspoon sugar
    2 eggs, beaten
    1 15-ounce can fruit cocktail
    ½ cup brown sugar
    ½ cup walnuts (or to taste)

Sauce:
    ⅔ cup half-and-half
    ¾ cup sugar
    ¾ cup margarine
    1 teaspoon vanilla

Preheat oven to 325 degrees. Combine flour, baking soda, sugar, eggs, and fruit cocktail in a bowl and beat together until blended. Pour into 9 x 13 inch glass baking dish. Sprinkle brown sugar and nuts over batter. Bake at 325 degrees for 55 minutes.

Remove from oven and let cool slightly while preparing sauce. Place half-and-half, sugar, margarine, and vanilla in small sauce pan and bring to a boil. Pour over warm cake.

Sugar

Lee Towata recalls the strict rationing during internment at Topaz, Utah, during World War II. One day, she was thrilled to receive a letter from her sister Nell telling her to expect a five-pound sack of sugar. Nell and her husband had moved to Oregon to work on a sugar beet farm. Lee eagerly awaited the arrival of the precious sugar! To her great dismay, when it finally arrived, it was soaked with gasoline. The sugar had been shipped with all kinds of other goods and the gasoline must have leaked and ruined the sugar. Lee is still a fabulous baker. Here is one of her recipes you might enjoy!

–Jo Takata

Sour Cream Muffins

 1 cup sour cream
 2 eggs, lightly beaten
 ¾ cup sugar
 1 teaspoon vanilla
 1 cup flour
 1 teaspoon baking powder
 1 teaspoon baking soda
 1 teaspoon salt

Preheat oven to 350 degrees. Mix together sour cream, eggs, sugar, and vanilla. Add dry ingredients and stir until combined. Spoon into muffin pans lined with paper cups. Bake for 20 minutes.

Makes 12 muffins

Frosted Carrot Cake

3 medium carrots, grated
1½ cups cooking oil
4 large eggs
2 cups flour
2 cups sugar
1 Tablespoon cinnamon
1 teaspoon allspice
2 teaspoons baking soda
2 teaspoons salt

Frosting:
1 box powdered sugar
8 ounces cream cheese
2 teaspoons vanilla

Preheat oven to 350 degrees. In a blender, combine oil, eggs, and carrots. Blend until mixed. Mix flour, sugar, spices, baking soda, and salt. Combine flour mixture and carrot mixture in a bowl. Pour into a 9 x 13 inch pan. Bake for 40 minutes or until knife is inserted and comes out clean. Cool before frosting. Mix frosting ingredients in bowl. Beat until smooth and easy to spread.

Pumpkin Pecan Dessert

  1 29-ounce can pumpkin
  1 14-ounce can evaporated milk
  1 cup sugar
  3 eggs
  2 teaspoons cinnamon
  1 18-ounce box yellow cake mix
  2 cubes butter, melted
  1 cup pecans, chopped
   Whipped cream or Cool Whip

Preheat oven to 350 degrees. Grease and flour a 9 x 13 inch pan. Mix first 5 ingredients together in a large bowl. Pour into pan. Sprinkle dried cake mix evenly on top. Pour melted butter on top of the mix. Cover with chopped pecans. Bake 60 minutes. Serve with whipped cream.

Pumpkin Roll

3 eggs
1 cup sugar
⅔ cup pumpkin
1 teaspoon vanilla
1 teaspoon baking soda
½ teaspoon salt
1 teaspoon cinnamon
¾ cup flour

Filling:

1 8-ounce package cream cheese
1 teaspoon vanilla
2 Tablespoons butter
1 cup powdered sugar

Preheat oven to 350 degrees. Mix eggs, sugar, pumpkin, and vanilla together in a large bowl for 5 minutes with an electric beater at medium speed. By hand, sift baking soda, salt, cinnamon, and flour together and add gradually to the pumpkin mixture. Line a 13 x 9 inch jelly roll pan with buttered waxed paper. Pour dough into the pan and bake for 15 minutes. Combine the filling ingredients and mix until smooth. After baking is completed, cut across the length of pan to get 2 rolls. Flip cake onto a dish towel and peel off wax paper. Flip cake again to have topside facing up. Roll warm cake into a roll with waxed paper or cloth to cover. Keep rolled until cooled. Gently unroll cake, spread filling inside, and re-roll. Freeze or refrigerate. Once the roll is set, cut into slices.

Serves 8 to 10

This dessert is more a Hawai'ian adaptation of the American classic cheesecake, incorporating sweet potatoes and haupia (coconut pudding), both luau staples. It is a relatively new concoction that has become a favorite for pot lucks and family gatherings in Hawai'i.

– Maureen Iwahashi

Sweet Potato Cheesecake With Haupia Frosting

Crust:
- 1 cup butter or margarine
- 2 cups flour
- ⅓ cup powdered sugar
- 1 egg yolk, reserving egg white for filling

Filling:
- 1 pound cream cheese at room temperature
- 3 eggs and reserved egg white from crust
- ¾ cup sugar
- 1 teaspoon vanilla
- 2 cups dark purple sweet potatoes, overcooked and mashed

Haupia:
- 4 cups coconut milk (2 cans, 12 ounces each; add water to make 4 cups)
- 1¼ cups sugar
- 1½ cups water
- ¾ cup cornstarch

Preheat oven to 350 degrees. Combine flour and sugar in bowl. Cut in butter until mixture is the texture of fine crumbs. Work in egg yolk with hands to make pliable dough. Spread into bottom of 9 x 13 inch baking pan with fingertips. Bake for 20 to 25 minutes until light brown.

Combine filling ingredients in bowl and mix until smooth. Pour over baked crust. Bake for 50 minutes; test with fork for doneness. Fork should come out somewhat clean. Cool about 15 minutes, then top with haupia frosting.

For frosting, bring coconut milk and sugar to boil in sauce pan. Separately, mix cornstarch and water. Slowly stir cornstarch mixture into coconut milk. Lower heat and cook until smooth and glossy, stirring constantly. Pour over semi-cooled sweet potato filling. Chill.

GLOSSARY

Every effort was made to include words our readers would need to successfully navigate the Japanese stores and products in search of ingredients for tasty meals.

Abura age or *Age:* Fried bean curd

Aemono: Salad

Agemono: Fried foods

Ajinomoto: Monosodium glutamate, MSG

Aka miso: Fermented red bean paste

An: Sweet red bean paste. There are two types, koshi'an (strained) and tsubushi'an (partially mashed)

Ankake: Dish with thickened sweet shōyu sauce

Araimo: Also satoimo. Japanese taro or dasheen

Asari: Also kogai, small clam

Atsuyaki tamago: Rolled fried eggs, Japanese style

Awabi: Abalone

Awase miso: Mixture of red (dark) and white (light) miso

Awase zu: Seasoned vinegar; vinegar-sugar-salt mixture for making sushi rice

Azuki: Japanese red beans

Bancha: Coarse Japanese green tea

Beni shōga: Red pickled ginger

Bentō: Japanese boxed lunch

Bok choy: Chinese cabbage; looks like Swiss chard

Botamochi or ohagi: Mochi rice ball covered with bean paste (An)

Buri: Yellowtail (fish)

Buta: Pork

Cha shu or char siu: Barbecued pork

Chawan: Rice bowl

Chawan mushi: Steamed egg custard dish

Chikuwa: Cylindrical fish cake

Chirashizushi: Seasoned rice with vegetables and/or seafood

Daikon: Japanese white radish

Daikon oroshi: Grated white radish

Dango: Dumpling

Dashi: Japanese soup stock made with kelp or dried bonito flakes. Instant dashi can be purchased in packets or jars.

Dashi konbu: Dried kelp for soup stock

Deba: Large vegetable chopping knife

Dobu: Curing mash for Japanese pickling

Donabe: Earthenware pot

Donburi: Covered bowl; rice dish with topping and sauce

Dorayaki: Small pancakes with azuki filling

Ebi: Prawn, shrimp

Edamame: Soybeans in pod, packaged frozen

Endō: Green peas

Enokidake: Long-stemmed white mushroom

Fu: Gluten cake

Fuki: Butterbur, coltsfoot

Funyū: Chinese fermented bean curd

Furikake: Seasoned seaweed topping

Ginnan: Gingko nut

Gobō: Burdock root

Gohan: Cooked rice

Goma: Sesame seed; two types kuro (black) goma and shiro (white) goma

Goma abura: Sesame oil

Goma shio or *gomajio:* Sesame seed with salt

Gomame or *tazukuri:* Small dried fish cooked in sugar-shōyu sauce

Gu: Ingredients

Gyōza: Filled dumpling, fried or steamed

Gyuhi: Mochi-type dessert

Hakusai, makina, or *napa:* Chinese cabbage

Hamaguri: Clam

Hana katsuo: Dried bonito flakes

Hana sansho: Japanese condiment

Hanbo or *handai:* Wooden container for mixing sushi rice

Hangiri daikon: Dried radish slices

Harusame: Thin yam or ming bean noodles

Hashi: Chopsticks

Hasu or renkon: Lotus root

Hawai'ian salt: Coarse sea salt

Hijiki: Slivered, dried seaweed

Hiya yakko: Cold tōfu served cut in squares

Hōchō: Japanese knife

Hoisin: Spicy bean sauce

Hokkigai: Clam

Hōrensō: Spinach

Iidako: Baby octopus

Ika: Squid

Inarizushi: Seasoned rice wrapped in seasoned bean curd (aburage)

Iriko: Small dried fish

Ise ebi: Lobster

Jagaimo: Irish potato

Jōshinko: Rice flour

Jūbako: Tiered lacquered box for picnic lunches

Kabayaki: Broiled with teriyaki-like sauce

Kabocha: Japanese squash

Kabu: Turnip

Kaibashira: Scallops

Kaki: Oyster

Kamaboko: Steamed fish cake

Kamameshi: Rice cooked in pot with other ingredients

Kani: Crab

Kanpyō: Dried gourd strips

Kanten: Agar agar

Karashi: Mustard

Karashi miso: Mustard miso

Kashiwa no ha: Oak leaves

Kasu: Sake lees (dregs)

Katakuriko: Potato starch

Katsuo: Bonito

Katsuobushi: Dried bonito or tuna flakes

Kayaku: Ingredients

Kazunoko: Herring roe

Kenchin: Tōfu and vegetables in soup

Kezurigatsuo: Shaved bonito flakes

Kibinago: Small frozen fish

Kikurage: Tree fungus; wood ear

Kim chee: Korean pickled vegetables

Kinako: Roasted soybean flour, light brown color

Kinpira: Stir fry with sugar-shōyu sauce

Kinshi tamago: Egg fried in thin sheets and julienned

Kinugoshi-dōfu: Soft-textured tōfu

Kirazu or okara: Bean curd residue

Kiri boshi or sengiri: Dried daikon strips

Kiri konbu: Finely cut seaweed

Kishimen: Wide flat noodles

Kome: Raw rice grains

Konbu: Dried seaweed

Konbu-maki: Dried seaweed rolled: tied with dried gourd stiprs (kanpyō)

Konnyaku: Firm translucent loaf made from the starch of devil's tongue plant tubers

Koromo: Tenpura batter

Kōyadōfu: Freeze-dried tōfu

Kuri: Chestnut

Kuro goma: Black sesame seeds

Kuromame: Dried black beans

Kurome: Fine seaweed

Kyūri: Cucumber

Long rice, or *sai fun:* cellophane noodles

Maguro: Tuna

Mai fun: Dried thin rice noodles

Makina: Won bok, napa cabbage

Manaita: Cutting board

Manjū: Rice flour pastry with azuki filling

Matsumae nori: Fine sheets of nori used in making barazushi

Matsutake: Fresh mountain pine mushrooms

Mirin: Sweet rice wine

Mirugai: King clam, gooeyduck

Miso: Fermented soybean paste

Misoni: Cooked with miso

Miso shiru: Bean paste soup

Mitsuba: Trefoil plant

Mizuame: Millet jelly

Mizutaki: Cooked in broth

Mochi: Glutinous (sweet) rice cake. Can be purchased frozen and ready to use

Mochigome: Glutinous rice

Mochiko: Sweet rice flour

Moyashi: Bean sprouts

Myōga: Myōga ginger flowers

Nabe: Pot or food prepared in a nabe

Namako: Sea cucumber

Nameko: Tiny, slippery mushrooms

Nanten: Nandina; heavenly bamboo

Napa: Chinese cabbage

Nasu or *nasubi:* Japanese eggplant

Negi: Green onions

Nigiri: Rice ball

Niku: Any meat

Nimono: Boiled food

Ninjin: Carrots

Ninniku: Garlic

Nira: Garlic chives

Nishime: Vegetables cooked in seasoned broth

Nori: Dried laver; seaweed

Norimaki: Sushi rolled in seaweed (nori)

Nuka: Rice bran

Obentō: Boxed lunch

Oboro: Dried flaked shrimp or fish

Ocha: Tea

Ochazuke: Rice with tea poured over it

Oden: Japanese stew in clear soup

Ohagi or *botamochi:* Mochi rice ball coated with red bean paste

Ohashi: Polite form of chopsticks (hashi)

Okara or *kirazu:* Bean curd residue

Okazu: Main dish with meat and vegetables

Okonomiyaki: Japanese pancake

Omoshi: Weight (press) used in preparing pickles

Osechi-ryōri: New Year's food

Osumashi: Clear soup

Otoshibuta: Drop-lid placed directly on simmering food

Owan: Lacquered soup bowl

Oyster sauce: Chinese seasoned sauce

Ozōni: New Year's mochi soup

Panko: Japanese bread crumbs

Ponzu: Vinegar or lemon and shōyu dressing or dipping sauce

Rakkyō or *rankyō:* Pickled scallions

Rangiri: Method of cutting vegetable by angle cutting at quarter turns

Renkon or *hasu:* Lotus root

Saba: Mackerel

Sai fun: Thin bean noodles

Sake: Japanese rice wine

Sanbaizu: Salt, sugar, and vinegar sauce

Sanma: Type of mackerel (pike)

Sanmai oroshi: Method of cutting fish removing the central bone, leaving two fillets

Sarashi negi: Green onions thinly sliced and chilled in water

Sashimi: Sliced, raw fish

Satoimo: Small taro potato

Satsuma-age: Fried fish cake

Sekihan: Rice cooked with red beans

Sengiri: Vegetables cut in strips

Shabu shabu: Beef cooked in broth

Shamoji: Rice ladle

Shichimi togarashi: Seven-spice pepper used with noodle dishes

Shiitake: Dried pine forest mushroom

Shimeji: A type of mushroom

Shioyaki: Broiled with salt

Shira ae: Food flavored with mashed tōfu

Shirasu boshi: Tiny white dried fish

Shirataki: Yam threads; konnyaku threads

Shiratamako: Rice powder

Shiro goma: White sesame seed

Shiromi: White fish

Shiro miso: White (light) miso

Shiromizu: Water in which rice has been washed

Shirona: Japanese spoon cabbage

Shiru: Sauce or soup

Shiso (Aka, red or Ao, green): Perilla; Beefsteak plant

Shōga: Ginger root

Shōga no amazuke: Sweet pickled ginger

Shōyu: Shōyu made from soy beans

Shungiku: Edible garland chrysanthemum leaves

Soba: Buckwheat noodles

Soboro: Fish or shrimp flakes; ground meat or chicken

Sōmen: Thin white noodles

Soramame: Broad beans; horse beans

Su: Vinegar

Sudare or *makisu:* Bamboo mat for rolling sushi

Suimono: Clear broth (soup)

Sukiyaki: Sliced meat with vegetables seasoned with sugar and shōyu

Sumashi: Clear broth

Sumiso: Vinegar-miso sauce

Sunomono: Vinegared salad

Suribachi: Serrated earthenware bowl for grinding

Surikogi: Wooden pestle for use with suribachi for grinding

Surimi: Fresh fish cake paste

Sushi: Vinegared rice

Sweet rice or *mochigome:* Short grain, glutinous rice

Tai: Sea bream

Takenoko: Bamboo shoots

Tako: Octopus

Takuwan: Picked Japanese radish

Tamago: Egg

Tamago usuyaki: Egg fried in thin sheets

Tamagoyaki: Omelet

Tamanegi: Round onions

Tarako: Codfish roe

Tare: Thickened, seasoned shōyu sauce

Tenpura: Deep fried food in light batter

Tentsuyu: Dipping sauce for tenpura

Teriyaki: Broiled food marinated with shōyu, sugar, and mirin or sake

Tōfu: Soybean curd

Tōgan: Chinese winter melon

Tonkatsu: Pork cutlet

Tori: Chicken

Toro: Oily belly part of tuna

Tsukejiru: Dipping sauce

Tsukemono: Pickled vegetables

Udon: Thick wheat flour noodles

Umani: Chicken and vegetables cooked in seasoned broth

Umeboshi: Pickled Japanese plum

Unagi: Eel

Uni: Sea urchin

Uri: A type of Japanese cucumber

Ushio: Clear soup

Wakame: Dried leafy seaweed

Warabi: Fernbrake or bracken

Warashita sauce: Sukiyaki flavoring sauce

Wasabi: Japanese horseradish

Won ton skins: Thin noodle-like dough cut into squares

Yakidōfu: Pan fried soybean curd cake

Yaki manjū: Baked pastry with azuki filling

Yamaimo: Japanese mountain yam

Yōkan: Sweetened bean paste confection

Yuzu: Rough-skinned citrus fruit

Zōsui: Rice cooked in soup

INDEX

PHOTO CREDIT

Front cover and Inside front and back cover

"Cooking for Work Crew," 1950,
courtesy of Setsu Kishi, National Japanese
American Historical Society

Back cover and page 22

"Child at Heston farm in Newton,
Pennsylvania," photo by Gretchen van Tassel,
National Archives, National Japanese
American Historical Society

Page 23

"Abalone Haul," Kodani Family Collection,
National Japanese American Historical Society

"Family," Courtesy of Patsy Iwasaki

"New Year's Table,"
Courtesy of Bess Yasukochi

Page 52

"Relocated to Chicago," 1944,
National Archives, National Japanese
American Historical Society

Page 53

"Home Fruit Company," Denver, Colorado,
March 1945, photo by Bud Aoyama,
National Archives, National Japanese
American Historical Society

"Strawberry Picker," National Archives,
National Japanese American Historical Society

"Girls with Chicks," San Jose, California, 1945,
photo by Hikaru Iwasaki, National Archives,
National Japanese American Historical Society

Page 94

"Living together in Cleveland, Ohio,"
National Archives, National Japanese
American Historical Society

Page 95

"Post War Apricot Harvest,"
National Archives, National Japanese
American Historical Society

"Community Picnic,"
National Archives, National Japanese
American Historical Society

"Chiyo Matsumiya and Balzly Family,"
courtesy of Jeanne Konishi

Page 111

"East First Street," Los Angeles, circa 1965,
photo by Toyo Miyatake, ©Archie Miyatake

Page 144

"Chick Sexing Advertisement,"
Scene, the Pictorial Magazine, Dec, 1951,
National Japanese American Historical Society

Page 160

"Fisherman," Kodani Family Collection,
National Japanese American Historical Society

The RICE COOKER'S COMPANION

Japanese American Food and Stories

ORDER FORM

Name _____

Address _____

City/State/Zip _____

Day/Evening Phone _____ Email _____

❑ I will pick up the book at the NJAHS office and will call first.

❑ Please mail the book(s) to the following address via first class mail.
(Add $4.00 per book for mailing/packaging costs)

❑ I want to order _____ cookbooks at $20.00 each $_____
NJAHS members 10% discount $_____
California residents add tax ($1.70 per book) $_____
$4.00 per book, shipping and handling $_____
TOTAL $_____

Ship to:

Name _____

Address _____

City/State/Zip _____

Please make checks payable to: NJAHS
1684 Post Street, San Francisco, CA 94115-3604

For more information, please call NJAHS at 415.921.5007, Fax at 415.921.5087,
or email at njahs@njahs.org. Thank you!